"With careful documentation from ancient writi
research, Jayson Georges reveals how the patron..
in which biblical authors lived and out of which they wrote. Jayson takes the reader through
multiple Old and New Testament passages revealing the patronage themes lodged within the
words, the people, and in the very situations. His examples reveal the complexity of patronage,
but readers experience clarity and simplicity throughout. Jayson's explanations of core doc-
trines (e.g., sin, salvation, atonement, love) are seen through the patron-client framework. The
case studies in the closing chapters provide helpful insights for doing ministry in patronage
cultures. I highly recommend Jayson's book as a worthy contribution to expand our understanding of the Scripture."

**Duane Elmer,** G. W. Aldeen Professor of International Studies, retired, Trinity International
University, author of *Cross-Cultural Connections*

"The African world, like the Middle Eastern and Asian contexts from which Jason writes, is
fraught with major social paradoxes. People often ask, Why is this country so corrupt if there
are so many Christians? Intractable contradictions such as corruption, ethnocentrism, clien-
telism, and related social pathologies are often cited to condescend Christian witness. While
Jayson neither essentializes (stereotypes) nor flattens out (generalizes) these issues any more
than African and Asian Christians condone them, cultivating an understanding of the causa-
tions and correlations between such problems and patronage reduces the particular stigmas
often ascribed to whole societies. As Christian ministers, if we can understand collocations
and convergences of cultural tendencies that we find deeply distressing, we are better placed
to discern redemptive opportunities to engage in transformative action. Jayson is leading us
toward that redemptive discernment."

**Wanjiru M. Gitau,** author of *Megachurch Christianity Reconsidered: Millennials and Social Change in
African Perspective*

"Jayson Georges has established himself as an important interdisciplinary and crosscultural
thinker. In this new book, he draws upon classical studies, biblical studies, modern cultural
anthropology, Christian theology, and his own (and others') first-hand missionary experience,
offering a comprehensive introduction to patronage in ancient and modern contexts and its
implications for biblical theology and missionary practice. He does this in engagingly accessible
and clear prose—and with winsome vulnerability as he recounts his own journey. This is an
important contribution to articulating a global gospel and formulating effective strategies for
serving and partnering with the global Christian community."

**David A. deSilva,** professor of New Testament at Ashland Theological Seminary and author of
*Honor, Patronage, Kinship & Purity*

"Whether you're serving in a crosscultural location or studying the Scriptures, Jayson
Georges's *Ministering in Patronage Cultures* will transform your understanding of patronage.
Because patron-client relationships dominate the majority of the world's population,
Georges's book fills a critical gap of knowledge. Furthermore, most of the people in the Bible
lived under this model of authority and relationship, hence a grasp of patronage is necessary
for proper biblical hermeneutics. . . . *Ministering in Patronage Cultures* guides, and ulti-
mately redeems, the patron-client orientation into a collaborative, interdependent, and
biblical model of patronage."

**Sharon Hoover,** director of missions, Centreville Presbyterian Church, VA, and author of *Mapping
Church Missions*

"Gaining a better understanding of patronage is reason enough to read this book. But it offers so much more than tips on how to better navigate patron-client relationships. Jayson Georges uses cultural insights to illuminate biblical texts and enrich theological understandings. Then, looking at patron-client relationships through a biblical lens Georges challenges us to practice transformed patronage. Read it and grow in knowledge of God and gain tools for God's mission."

**Mark D. Baker,** professor of mission and theology, Fresno Pacific Biblical Seminary

"Few subjects are as significant yet overlooked as patronage is. Many Westerners are suspicious of patronage, assuming it leads only to corruption. In *Ministering in Patronage Cultures*, Jayson Georges removes the cloud of confusion that surrounds the topic. With characteristic clarity, Georges sheds light on the ways that patronage influences culture, shapes biblical theology, and should transform our ministries. I highly recommend *Ministering in Patronage Cultures*. No book like this one exists."

**Jackson W.,** author of *Reading Romans with Eastern Eyes*

"In crosscultural ministry, patronage is often the elephant in the room. If you are ministering to people who are not of European descent, then it is highly likely you are working with collectivists; yet, many of us Westerners are individualists. For collectivists, patronage is the air they breathe, the water they swim in. It is what goes without being said. Abandon any foolish notion of avoiding patronage. . . . As Georges notes, patronage is biblical. Come along with Jayson Georges as he teaches us how patronage, like all aspects of culture, may be warped by sin but can and should be redeemed for kingdom work. I enthusiastically commend this book to anyone wanting to serve those who come from the Majority World. . . . Georges is an experienced and skilled guide, patiently tutoring us individualists on how to minister in a collectivist world."

**E. Randolph Richards,** Palm Beach Atlantic University, coauthor of *Misreading Scripture with Western Eyes*

"If you see the world and the gospel as I do, through the lens of an egalitarian, democratic, individualistic worldview, and you desire to communicate crossculturally to people from the Majority World, then Jayson Georges is a voice you must hear. *Ministering in Patronage Cultures* will expand your understanding of the Scriptures, intensify your crosscultural understanding, and enlarge your capacity to worship responsively as a redeemed servant of Jesus Christ."

**Paul Borthwick,** senior consultant for Development Associates International, author of *Western Christians in Global Mission*

"Jayson Georges brings out the nuances of patronage in an articulate manner. An eloquent storyteller, Jayson draws out principles of applying patronage in ministry with expert insight, relevant examples, and appropriate biblical proofs. Having ministered among Muslims for twenty-four years and realizing that understanding patronage is vital to ministering among honor-shame cultures, I highly recommend this book for everyone who is currently or even planning to minister, live, or do business in or with patronage cultures."

**Syed Ibn Syed,** missionary to Muslims in the Arabian Peninsula, author of *Try Me, I Am Jesus*

# MINISTERING
## *in* PATRONAGE
# CULTURES

### BIBLICAL MODELS *and*
### MISSIONAL IMPLICATIONS

## JAYSON GEORGES

**Academic**

An imprint of InterVarsity Press
Downers Grove, Illinois

*InterVarsity Press*
*P.O. Box 1400, Downers Grove, IL 60515-1426*
*ivpress.com*
*email@ivpress.com*

*InterVarsity Press® is the book-publishing division of InterVarsity Christian Fellowship/USA®, a
movement of students and faculty active on campus at hundreds of universities, colleges, and schools
of nursing in the United States of America, and a member movement of the International Fellowship
of Evangelical Students. For information about local and regional activities, visit intervarsity.org.*

*Scripture quotations, unless otherwise noted, are from the New Revised Standard Version of the Bible,
copyright 1989 by the Division of Christian Education of the National Council of the Churches of Christ
in the USA. Used by permission. All rights reserved.*

*While any stories in this book are true, some names and identifying information may have been
changed to protect the privacy of individuals.*

*Cover design: David Fassett*
*Interior design: Daniel van Loon*
*Images: bright blue galaxy: © Sololos / E+ / Getty Images*
*    bright abstract background: © oxygen / Moment Collection / Getty Images*

*ISBN 978-0-8308-5247-5 (print)*
*ISBN 978-0-8308-7089-9 (digital)*

*Printed in the United States of America ♾*

*InterVarsity Press is committed to ecological stewardship and to the conservation of natural resources
in all our operations. This book was printed using sustainably sourced paper.*

**Library of Congress Cataloging-in-Publication Data**
*A catalog record for this book is available from the Library of Congress.*

| **P** | 25 | 24 | 23 | 22 | 21 | 20 | 19 | 18 | 17 | 16 | 15 | 14 | 13 | 12 | 11 | 10 | 9 | 8 | 7 | 6 | 5 | 4 | 3 | 2 | 1 |
|---|---|---|---|---|---|---|---|---|---|---|---|---|---|---|---|---|---|---|---|---|---|---|---|---|---|
| **Y** | 37 | 36 | 35 | 34 | 33 | 32 | 31 | 30 | 29 | 28 | 27 | 26 | 25 | 24 | 23 | 22 | 21 | 20 | 19 |

*To Mom and Dad,*

*models of generosity*

# CONTENTS

# ACKNOWLEDGMENTS

IN WRITING ABOUT RECIPROCITY AND GRATITUDE, I find myself indebted to many people. This book has benefited greatly from the contributions of other people. This section merely acknowledges my debt to them, for repayment is hardly possible. If only I could build a monument to honor their benevolence!

I'm thankful for the organizations that provided a venue to teach and discuss patronage around the world—Frontiers, EthneCity, VisionSynergy, World Team, YWAM, Encompass World Partners, and Eternity Bible College. I learned a great deal from those conversations.

I also wish to thank the people who read the manuscript and provided instructive feedback. This includes Mark Baker, Jackson W., Jon Marshall, David Briones, Duke Dillard, David deSilva, Robert and Anne Theissen, and my editor, Anna Gissing.

The Patronage Symposium hosted in Beirut, Lebanon (2018) generated three days of rich discussions and insights. A special thanks to all the presenters and participants—our time together helped me clarify and sharpen many aspects of my final draft.

I am also thankful for amazing ministry teammates. Your lives modeled for me the nature of biblical relationships. And thanks to my wife and girls, who are always abounding in generosity. I thank God for you, the most precious of gifts.

# INTRODUCTION

## *The Problems of Patronage*

I ALWAYS DREADED SEEING ALISHER ON THE STREET. He was a great guy, but he always did something that made me feel awkward. Alisher was the government official who oversaw our neighborhood in Central Asia. With an entrepreneurial personality, he assumed responsibility to help meet needs in the community. So Alisher often asked our family for help, and we gave whenever possible. But over time, our interactions became awkward. Whenever I encountered Alisher on the street, he eagerly found a bystander to whom he could boast of my contributions. "When the children have needs," he proclaimed, "Jayson always helps! He gave computers to our office. His business employs many people! His organization pays for a basketball league!" For me as a Westerner, his incessant praise felt uncomfortable, even embarrassing. Why was Alisher publicizing my contributions to other people? What did that accomplish in his mind?

Ted and Vicky were American Christians who served in Afghanistan. They found it difficult to give money to people in a helpful manner. Giving charity to a beggar sometimes led to a mob of people demanding money. But giving a loan often broke the relationship because the borrower would disappear to avoid the shame of being unable to repay. One day Ted and Vicky received money from American friends to help their poor neighbor Hamida. They considered the best way to help and decided to anonymously pay off her family's large debt at the local market. Ted asked the shopkeeper, a good friend, not to share with anyone what they were doing. But the next day, Hamida burst into their house and demanded they get the money back from the shopkeeper. She feared the neighbors would find out and call her family "beggars," thus ruining their reputation. After that incident, neighbors approached Ted and Vicky on the street with honey-sweet greetings, asking them to come visit their homes. For Westerners and Afghanis, finances play a very different role in relationships. But why? What are the unmentioned expectations?

In Luke 16, Jesus tells a strange story to his disciples. A man was dishonest at work, so his boss fired him from the job. Before word spread about his misdeeds throughout the community, he cut secret deals with all the people who owed his boss money—"Just give me half of what you owe, and I will give you a receipt showing you paid in full." When the boss found out about these secret deals, he commended his dishonest employee! Why would Jesus tell a story that praises someone for financial deceit? How should we understand Jesus' ethic of money and relationships?

These three stories portray a stark reality—cultures approach money and relationships very differently. In many cultures of the world, patronage functions as the social "operating system" that shapes relationships. In the paradigm of patronage, rich people are expected to help meet material needs, and the receiver is obligated to repay with honor. These expectations of patronage are culturally hardwired into the societies in which Alisher, Hamida, and Jesus lived. But unfortunately, Westerners are hardly aware of this cultural reality, and this creates problems at various levels. Since patronage is how collectivistic societies operate, understanding patron-client relationships helps unlock the nuances of global cultures and biblical texts.

An American missionary in Southeast Asia commented to me, "I feel like everyone sees a big *P* [for *patron*] stamped on my forehead!" The problem though is that most Westerners are unaware of the big "P." An Asian American missiologist notes,

> In many cases, Westerners who have been taught equality, and the virtues of independence in their culture, are not prepared to understand the intricate rules and expectations of Patron-Client relationships. They are not conscious of their expected role as patrons.[1]

Western missionaries are unprepared, both culturally and biblically, to handle issues related to patronage in their relationships. They misjudge

---

[1]Robert Oh, "Patron-Client Dynamics Between Korean Missionaries and Cambodian Christians," *Asia Missions Advance* 48 (July 2015): 15.

relationships and stumble through financial situations. Patronage causes confusion and frustration. The dynamics of patronage have strained the joy out of their relationships and have even caused missionaries to prematurely leave their field of ministry.

Patronage creates problems not only for Westerners ministering in other cultures but also for any modern person who reads the Bible. Reading Scripture means entering a different culture and social world. If we ignore the pivotal values of patronage in biblical cultures, we will misinterpret Yahweh's relationship with Israel, Jesus' parables, and Paul's letters. The concept of patronage, as this book explains, is an essential construct for interpreting biblical stories, developing a robust theology, and even worshiping God. Patronage is not just a cultural or missiological issue but also a profoundly biblical and theological one. For me personally, learning about patronage in the Bible and writing this book has significantly reshaped my own theology and spirituality. My heart has grown more inclined to thanking God as my benevolent Patron. A biblical perspective on patronage reframes our relationship with God and adds depth to theological concepts such as faith, grace, and salvation.

Here is our roadmap toward developing a biblical perspective on patronage.

Chapters 1–3 address *cultural issues* regarding patronage. What is patronage and how does it work? How is patronage expressed in relationships? Why exactly is patronage so frustrating for Westerners? These chapters develop a general cultural model of patronage while also observing some ways patronage can vary across cultures. This framework helps us understand the primary socioeconomic system of Majority World and biblical cultures.

Chapters 4–6 examine *biblical models* of patronage. How did biblical figures engage relationships in a patronage culture? Yahweh, Jesus, and Paul did not reject the cultural system. They adopted and transformed patronage for kingdom purposes. Biblical patronage, as we see in their examples, is God-centered and life-giving.

Chapters 7–9 articulate *theological concepts* in light of patronage. How does patronage illuminate our theology of God, salvation, and sin? Since patronage dominated the social world of first-century Christians, it significantly shapes New Testament theology. Patronage helps explain the very nature of the gospel and our relationship with God.

Chapters 10–12 unpack the *missional applications* of biblical patronage. How and when should Christians engage in patron-client relationships? Which positive elements can be adopted? How should negative elements be transformed? How can we make our patronage relationships more God-centered and life-giving? How does patronage apply to our personal lives and ministries? A biblical paradigm of patronage has profound implications for relationships today.

## SOME EXPLANATIONS

In writing this book about patronage, I repeatedly faced three challenges: relationships are complex, cultures are unique, and English is inadequate. I explain these challenges and my provisional solutions because readers will face similar obstacles as they think about patronage.

First, the relational dynamics surrounding patronage are complex. Many missionaries have faced a situation like this: "A disciple-friend asks me for $20 to buy new shoes for his son, and I reflexively think, *He spent two days helping me find a car part, so I do owe him . . . but he still owes me $50 from three months ago . . . plus I've been teaching him about finances to avoid this very problem . . . and I just recently declined to help another church member with a similar request . . . and the money might be to buy a gift for the dean of his son's university . . . what should I do!?*"

In reality, patronage relationships involve many factors and layers. The complexity of "financial friendships" defies simple rules for crosscultural relationships. This book incorporates biblical teaching, real stories, and practical advice to establish general *principles* (not rules). A better understanding of patronage in cultural contexts and Scripture allows us to better engage patronage relationships with great fruitfulness.

Second, patronage takes on a unique shape in every culture. There is not a one-size-fits-all model of patronage for every culture. My comments about patronage are simply generalizations—a description of the socio-economic similarities that *most* Majority World cultures share in common, especially when compared to Western cultures.

Understanding patronage means balancing the tension between broad generalizations and particular expressions. This book presents a general model for patronage but also features case studies from many countries around the world—Afghanistan, Cambodia, Cameroon, China, Haiti, Honduras, Kyrgyzstan, Malawi, the Philippines, Russia, Thailand, and the United States. I also discuss patronage in ancient cultures like biblical Israel, the Greco-Roman empire, and medieval Europe. The general framework for patronage describes tendencies that are generally true of collectivistic, honor-shame oriented cultures, while the case studies provide more texture and concrete nuance.

Third, the English language is a poor medium for discussing patronage. One day I went to the Department of Driver Services in Atlanta to register our family's car. After I paid the fees, the clerk handed me my receipt, which said in large font across the top, "Thank You for Your Patronage." In the market-based economies of the West, the word *patron* often refers to a customer. (Strangely, the English word *client* also means customer.) This popular meaning of *patron* in English is entirely different than the Majority World phenomenon of patronage discussed in this book.

Here is the issue. Patron-client relationships are far less prominent in the English-speaking cultures. Since words derive their meaning from social contexts, and the English language is not naturally used in contexts of patronage, English words fail to capture the nuance and depth of social dynamics related to reciprocal relationships. Discussing patronage in English is like using ancient Latin to explain the internet—the words are not meant for such a task. My solution in this book is to use a variety of terms that evoke patronage. These words at times do feel unnatural but seem to prove workable.

The system: *patronage, benefaction, clientage*

The giver: *patron, benefactor*

The motive: *generosity, kindness, beneficence, benevolence*

The object: *gift, favor, grace, benefit, benefaction*

The action: *to help, to provide benefaction, to gift*

The receiver: *client, beneficiary*

The expectation: *obligation, social debt, reciprocity, loyalty, allegiance, trustworthiness, faithfulness, gratitude, gratefulness, thankfulness*

A discussion on patronage can open a can of worms. The topic is controversial and prompts many questions, both theoretical and practical. To make this book concise and accessible I have intentionally avoided technical conversations. Readers who want to further engage patronage should consult the bibliography of further reading in Appendix 1. Readers seeking guidance for practical ministry should realize that a short book about a broad topic cannot solve every problem related to patronage. Rather than offering a three-step process, this book introduces a new paradigm and gives some positive examples and potential applications so that we can be more confident and creative in our ministries. In a way, learning to navigate patronage is like learning a new language—we learn best through practice and experience. Reading a book does not make us proficient in a new language, but it introduces the main points to enhance the learning process. We approach the topic of patronage as a new framework or skill for deeper relationships, not as a how-to method for instant results. With those qualifications in mind, let's discuss how patronage works.

# PART ONE

# CULTURAL ISSUES

# 1

# THE MEANING OF PATRONAGE

PATRONAGE, SIMPLY PUT, is a reciprocal relationship between a patron and a client. Patrons are the superior party with resources and power to help other people. Their favors and benefits take many forms, such as covering the hospital expenses for a sick person, hosting a feast, procuring the documents for a friend's business, allowing farmers to cultivate their fields, building a new road, etc. Patrons use their influence and wealth to ensure other people's security and survival. Their generosity protects and provides for the people under their care.

Clients, on the other hand, are social inferiors who attach themselves to a patron in order to secure protection and resources. To maintain the patronage relationship, clients must reciprocate when they receive help from the patron. But the client is not as wealthy as the patron, so instead of repaying financially, they repay by honoring the patron. A client offers obedience, gratitude, allegiance, and solidarity to the patron. Clients demonstrate their loyalty in a variety of ways—they vote for the patron running for public office, fight on the patron's behalf, offer public praise at any opportunity, offer token gifts, and do symbolic acts of service. These actions honor the patron. The client seeks to enhance the patron's reputation, often at great personal cost, hoping such loyalty will be rewarded by the generous patron. Figure 1.1 visualizes the reciprocal relationship between patrons and clients.

Patrons are the "haves," clients are the "have-nots," and patronage is when the "haves" solve the problems for the "have-nots." The patron provides for the client's material needs, and the client meets the patron's desires for social status. Paul Hiebert explains,

The patron, like a parent, is totally responsible for the welfare of his clients. . . . Clients in fact can ask a patron for whatever they think he may grant, but this is not considered begging—no more than Christians think they are begging when they ask God for help. Clients for their part, must be totally loyal to their patron. . . . The patron gains power and prestige within the society, and the client gains security.[1]

Patronage is generally defined as a "reciprocal, asymmetrical relationship."[2] Each word in this definition denotes a crucial aspect of patronage. First, patronage is a *relationship*, not some legal arrangement. Patronage involves an enduring parent and child type of commitment, not a one-time financial contribution or business deal. The exchange of resources creates and cultivates an ongoing relationship. But to their own peril, Westerners mistakenly "describe the relationships between a patron and a client as contractual, like a business, rather than as familial."[3]

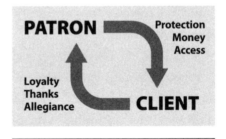

**Figure 1.1.** The patronage relationship

Also, the relationship of patronage is *reciprocal*. There is a mutual exchange of resources. Each side in the relationship gives something, whether material (e.g., money, protection) or social (e.g., loyalty, praise). There is an expectation, perhaps even a moral obligation, that the receiver will repay the debt. Each side benefits because the other side gives, and this creates an ongoing reciprocity that deepens the relationship.

---

[1]Paul G. Hiebert, *Anthropological Insights for Missionaries* (Grand Rapids: Baker Academic, 1986), 124.

[2]This definition follows from the work of classicist and Roman historian Richard P. Saller, *Personal Patronage Under the Early Empire* (Cambridge: Cambridge University Press, 1982). His has become the standard definition of patronage among sociocultural historians of ancient and modern societies, as well as New Testament scholars.

[3]E. Randolph Richards and Brandon J. O'Brien, *Misreading Scripture with Western Eyes: Removing Cultural Blinders to Better Understand the Bible* (Downers Grove, IL: InterVarsity Press, 2012), 162.

Finally, these reciprocal relationships are *asymmetrical,* or unequal. The patron has a higher social status than the client. They are not peers. The difference in status is an inherit aspect of the patron-client relationship.[4] Patronage allows unequals to interact and exchange resources in a mutually beneficial manner, but without jeopardizing their social distinction. In summary, the core features of patronage are relationship, reciprocity, and asymmetry.

## KEY ASPECTS OF PATRONAGE

The system of patronage is not a simple mechanical procedure but the interaction of various social dynamics working together to enhance social bonds and facilitate exchanges. Here are common characteristics of relationships in patronage cultures: social pyramids, superiority/inferiority, relational imbalance, mediation, power brokers, social capital, clout, gifts, connections, reciprocity, obligations, "friends," loyalty, generosity, benevolence, favoritism, honor, and shame. From this list, three particular aspects—social capital, brokers, and honor—propel the cycle of patron-client exchanges. So we examine them in more depth.

***Social capital.*** Western economies mostly use financial currency to exchange goods and resources. If you buy a jacket at Target, you pay twenty-five dollars in cash. If you rent a room through Hotels.com, you pay seventy-nine dollars with your credit card. An American can make dozens of transactions in a single day but exit each interaction without any relational obligation. Paying money absolves our (social) debt, and the receipt confirms our independence from the seller.

In contrast, Majority World cultures often use a different currency to exchange resources. People in reciprocal relationships barter "social capital." For example, if you host a lunch, you accrue two credits of social capital. If you built a new stadium in town, then you'd get one hundred credits! Of course, there are no physical receipts or monthly statements in the system of patronage; people track account balances in their minds. The Turkish people have a proverb about hospitality: "The memory of one tea lasts forty

---

[4]Robert Oh, "Patron-Client Dynamics Between Korean Missionaries and Cambodian Christians," *Asia Missions Advance* 48 (July 2015): 14.

years." People invest their resources (e.g., time, labor, gifts, marriageable children) to accrue a more positive social status. When relationships are essential for getting resources, a person's reputation and social capital are immensely valuable assets.

According to sociologist Pierre Bourdieu, social capital is the ability to access resources through social networks and relationships. A person's social capital "depends on the size of the network of connections he can effectively mobilize and on the volume of the capital."[5] Relationships equal wealth. Compared to financial capital, social capital is an intangible currency, for it only exists within the context of specific relationships and communities.

The Chinese concept of *guanxi* is an example of social capital. The word *guanxi* refers to a person's network of mutually beneficial relationships, particularly in the business world. People maintain the socioeconomic order by relating with others in a hierarchical fashion. Such *guanxi* networks are built upon mutual obligations, relational trust, and implicit reciprocity. Leveraging *guanxi* in business is not considered bribery but is actually expected. People feel obliged to trade favors and cooperate with others in their *guanxi* network of relationships. This is the nature of social capital.

***Brokers.*** Ricardo grew up playing music in Ecuador. One day he was invited to play drums for a band that was organized by the sons of a police colonel. The band had a great show, and Ricardo became part of that family band. Over time his relationship with the family deepened, and he became one of them. In a country where danger abounds, having a police colonel as a friend was helpful. For Ricardo that meant they would help anytime he needed. So once Ricardo's relatives learned about his relationship with the colonel's family, they had a new level of respect for him. Ricardo's family viewed him as a "broker" who could connect them to the police colonel and thus help ensure their safety and security. Without some intermediary, Ricardo's family could not gain access to the powerful police colonel.

---

[5]Pierre Bourdieu, "The Forms of Capital," in *Education: Culture, Economy, and Society*, ed. A. H. Halsey et al. (New York: Oxford University Press, 1997), 51.

The social gap between patrons and clients can be extreme, and thus insurmountable. Lowly clients cannot directly approach powerful patrons. Bridging the social gap requires a "broker," a trusted intermediary who links the two parties together. "By possessing strategic contact with the wealthy, the broker bridges the social chasm between patron and client in a way that is profitable for both parties."[6] The term *broker* is not an official title, but a general description for people who use connections to facilitate access. Brokers know somebody who can help. By facilitating the exchange between patron and client, the broker accrues honor. In the end, brokerage creates a winning situation for all three parties—patron, broker, and client.

Recall the story of Elisha and the wealthy Shunammite woman who provided patronage for Elisha's itinerant ministry (2 Kings 4). Whenever Elisha passed through town, she provided a meal, and she even built a furnished bedroom for Elisha (2 Kings 4:8-10). Though she never asked for any favors, Elisha offered to reciprocate. "Since you have taken all this trouble for us, what may be done for you? Would you have a word spoken on your behalf to the king or to the commander of the army?" (2 Kings 4:13). To repay her generosity, Elisha offered to mediate access to the ruling powers. Elisha presented himself as a broker in the system of patronage.

The nuances of brokerage create a web of relationships with fluid social roles. For example, a broker functions as both patron and client. To the superior person, the broker is a special yet subservient client. And for the inferior person, the broker is the functional patron who provides access to benefits and so deserves gratitude. As a result, society functions as an interlocking network of obligations and social bonds. Aspects of patronage, brokerage, and clientage become woven into all social relationships. The relational connectivity of these patronage networks stabilizes and defines the community.

***Honor (and shame).*** Patronage is a system for acquiring honor. The sharing of resources converts financial assets into social status. The wealthy share money to gain honor. In ancient Greco-Roman society, patronage allowed people

---

[6]David Briones, "Mutual Brokers of Grace: A Study in 2 Corinthians 1.3-11," *NTS* 56, no. 4 (October 2010): 543.

to accrue honor, status and worth for oneself and before others. . . . For a person's self-estimation as worthy (*dignus*) to become a social-estimation, it had to be confirmed by those whose opinion mattered. One way to achieve this honorific outcome, as least within elite circles, was by displaying one's social worth through acts of generosity.[7]

In fact, the Greek word *philotimia* (literally, "love of honor") was a word for public benefaction.[8] Patrons obtain social prominence by publicly displaying their fortune. This pursuit of honor and glory propelled the system of patronage.

Patronage increases a person's honor in two ways. First, exchanging resources solidifies a person's relational network. Gifts form and enhance social bonds. And in cultures that measure status by who a person knows, those social bonds enhance status. In other words, acts of patronage create a network of clients, which increases a patron's honor. "The patron gains honor through the widespread knowledge that he can sustain a large body of clients."[9]

Second, patronage demonstrates that a person is relationally trustworthy, which is a prominent character virtue. Since patronage is not enforced with legal contracts or written agreements, people invest in relationships only with trustworthy people. As a person fulfills the expectations of patronage, their trustworthiness increases, which in turn allows access to more relationships which means more status. Patrons (and clients) who "stay true" and "keep faith" gain honor.

Along with the carrot of honor, the stick of shame also motivates patronage. Communities use shame to pressure the patrons into sharing resources. The failure of a rich person to share resources is a cardinal disgrace in collectivistic cultures. A missionary in West Africa explained to me, "The worst sin here is to have money and not share it with others. You can be a thief, a drunkard, or a fornicator and society may forgive you, but not if you are ungenerous."[10] Failing to be a patron as the community expects

---

[7]David Briones, *Paul's Financial Policy: A Socio-Theological Approach* (London: Bloomsbury T&T Clark, 2015), 134-35.

[8]Joan Cecelia Campbell, *Phoebe: Patron and Emissary* (Collegeville, MN: Liturgical Press, 2009), 86.

[9]T. Raymond Hobbs, "Reflections on Honor, Shame, and Covenant Relations," *JBL* 116, no. 3 (1997): 502.

[10]Interview with a missionary conducted in Yaoundé, Cameroon, May 2016.

brings tremendous disgrace. Dio Chrysostom, a rich politician in first century Rome, encountered this social reality. During a grain shortage, a mob accused him of not sharing his wealth with the community. The citizens singled him out for dishonor, threatening to stone and burn him. Note the logic: when the rich do not share, they deserve shame. Patrons in ancient Rome gave help in order to curry favor and win public office. Once elected, they faced pressure to continue being generous. Client-voters used the threat of shame to exert pressure on their patron-politicians.[11] Dio Chrysostom defended himself by citing examples of his generous and honorable behavior. He boasts that he did not deprive his poor neighbors of their possessions or evict them from their small holdings, as less benevolent politicians might have done. Through such benevolence he managed to avoid shame (*Or.* 46:7-8).

The threat of shame also propels clients to respond properly. Clients must return favors with thanks. Ungrateful clients who do not reciprocate are dis-graced, i.e., removed from favor(s). They are shamed as unworthy recipients. In light of these honor-shame dynamics, we could summarize the moral calculus of patronage relationships as such:

- Patrons gain honor by being generous and are shamed for being stingy.
- Clients gain honor by being loyal and are shamed for being ungrateful.

## THE MORALITY OF PATRONAGE

For many cultures, the reciprocal generosity of patronage is a moral obligation. Patrons *must* give favors and clients *must* give thanks, lest they jeopardize their own reputation and the unifying fabric of society. So when an affluent person fails to follow the prescribed role of patron, he or she "is considered cold and uncaring and unsuitable as a patron."[12] For the recipients, gratitude is also a moral category. The failure to respond in thanks indicates a moral deficiency. Gifts create a new condition, a new relationship

---

[11]Halvor Moxnes, "Patron-Client Relations and the New Community in Luke-Acts," in *The Social World of Luke-Acts: Models for Interpretation*, ed. Jerome H. Neyrey (Peabody, MA: Hendrickson, 1991), 249.

[12]Paul DeNeui, "Speaking of the Unspeakable: Money and Missions in Patron-Client Buddhist Cultures," in *Complexities of Money and Mission in Asia*, ed. Paul DeNeui (Pasadena, CA: William Carey Library, 2012), 110.

that must be properly acknowledged. In these ways the dynamics of patronage and social reciprocity are innately moral.

Dr. Richard Shweder, a professor of cultural psychology at the University of Chicago, researches the moral reasoning of cultures around the world. His explanation of morality in non-Western societies is essentially patronage. Collectivistic cultures perceive ethics, he says, as

> obligations engendered through participation in a particular community. . . .
> Powerful persons take care of their "subjects": family members, employees,
> fellow cast members. Along with hierarchy there is an obligatory responsibility
> for others. The less powerful respond with gratitude and loyalty that "sticks"
> when the chips are down.[13]

Reciprocity is a moral obligation. Failing to give as one ought is ethically wrong. There are no laws against stingy patrons or ungrateful clients, but there are obvious social consequences. The notion that "reciprocity = virtue" lies at the core of collectivistic cultures. In their minds, moral people know how to be good patrons and clients. For this reason, Greco-Roman philosophers like Aristotle, Cicero, and Seneca discussed benefaction in the context of ethics (not cultural anthropology). The opening words of Seneca's book about benefaction declare, "There is almost most nothing, I would claim, more harmful than our ignorance of how to give and receive benefits" (*Ben* 1.1.1). Ancient philosophers described patronage so that people would offer gifts and reciprocate in a virtuous, respectable manner.

The importance of generosity in Arab cultures illustrates the virtue of patronage and reciprocity. In Arabic, the same word *kareem* refers to both generosity and virtue. Arabs consider generosity to be the opposite of iniquity. The Arabic word for honor/dignity, *karameh*, comes from the same root as generosity. So to show generosity, in essence, is to possess honor. Generosity for Arabs is not a charitable act but a character virtue, something that reveals the core of who someone *is*.[14]

---

[13]Richard A. Shweder et al., "The 'Big Three' of Morality (Autonomy, Community, Divinity) and the 'Big Three' Explanations of Suffering," in *Morality and Health*, eds. A. M. Brandt and P. Rozin (New York: Routledge, 1997), 145-46.

[14]These insights are from Richard Yakoub, "The Amazingly Generous God" (unpublished paper, Lebanon, 2016), 2-3. Used with permission from author.

In sum, patronage is foremost a system of social ethics centered around relational loyalty and honor.[15] This of course does not imply that all forms of patronage are moral or honorable. Some people corrupt and manipulate the system for their own gain, as later chapters discuss.

## THE LANGUAGE OF PATRONAGE

While living in Central Asia I operated a small weight gym. One day a muscular wrestler approached me, saying, "Hey Jayson, let me be your 'roof'!" In Russian, *roof* is the slang word for "patron." His comment was a coded offer to protect my business from other thugs in exchange for free gym membership. Even though I knew what he meant, I was curious to learn more about his offer. So with a confused expression, I looked up at the ceiling and said, "But we already have a good roof. It has no leaks!" This forced him to spell out, rather sheepishly, what he meant by *roof*—someone who uses his strength and connections to protect others.

Cultures use various words for the concept of patron. Examples include *roof* (Russian), *shepherd* (Arabic), *backrest* (Cambodian), *shade* (Thai), *the first* (Korean), *lord* (medieval Europe), and even *savior* (ancient Greek). When referring to patrons, people typically use street-level euphemisms, not technical terms. Scholars recognize that patronage is "a general type of personal relationship that may occur in any society under widely different names and appearances."[16] For this reason, one must be aware of the local vocabulary for patrons, clients, and patronage to correctly understand and navigate patronage in local contexts. As you explore patronage dynamics in a specific context, look for the terms and metaphors that refer to the reality of patronage.

Contemporary literature uses various English terms for the phenomenon of patronage. "Patron," from the Latin *patronus*, has become a general sociological term, though the word originally meant a legal-defender in Roman society.[17] "Benefactor" is a Roman translation of the Greek term

---

[15]See E. Badian, *Foreign Clientelae (264-70 B.C.)* (Oxford: Oxford University Press, 1958). This work illustrates how client-states with Rome reflected the moral model of patronage.

[16]Koenraad Verboven, *The Economy of Friends: Economic Aspects of* Amicitia *and Patronage in the Late Republic* (Brussels: Latomus, 2002), 51.

[17]The term *patronage* comes from Roman history. In the Latin system of *clientela*, a *patronus* was a powerful aristocrat with loyal followers, *clientes*. Though Romans birthed language of patronage, they

*euergetōn*, which originally referred to a sponsor of public works, but is now broadly used as a synonym for patron. Old Testament scholars refer to ancient Near Eastern patron-kings as a *suzerain*, an etic term from the French word for "sovereign." In cultural anthropology, the phrase "big man" refers to an influential tribal leader. These terms are not exact synonyms, but all generally refer to the leader of a reciprocal, asymmetrical relationship. For the sake of simplicity, this book mostly uses the language of "patron/age" and "benefaction."

## THE CAUSES OF PATRONAGE

Why does patronage happen? How does patronage become the de facto system in a society? The two main causes of patronage are (1) socioeconomic inequality and (2) the lack of formal institutions.

Widespread economic inequality leads to patronage. Inequality means that a minority of people control most of the wealth and power. The elite live comfortably while the powerless live an impoverished existence on the margins. The poor are only one injury away from death or one failed crop away from utter ruin. Economic disparity means the poor face the constant threat of destitution unless they find some way to secure resources. The Roman politician Seneca said, "It is only through the interchange of benefits that life becomes in some measure equipped and fortified against sudden disasters" (*Ben.* 4.18.1).

Inequality alone does not necessitate patronage. For example, the United States is one of most wealth-unequal countries in the world,[18] yet patronage is not prevalent in America. The reason is because formal institutions in America allow access to key resources. For example, an insurance company may provide $100,000 to a family when a parent dies, the government gives

---

did not invent the system. Patronage was a widespread phenomenon before and beyond the Roman empire. In Latin, *patrocinium* was a technical term for protection and legal defense (not a broad description, like "benefaction"), and only a Roman citizen could be an official *patronus*. See, Jonathan Marshall, *Jesus, Patrons, and Benefactors: Roman Palestine and the Gospel of Luke* (Tübingen: Mohr Siebeck, 2009). However, contemporary anthropologists use the language of *patronage* as a general category for all hierarchical, reciprocal relationships across time and space. This anthropological meaning, not the technical Latin term, is used in this book.

[18] The income gap between CEOs and employees or the wealth gap between various races in America outpaces those of "developing countries."

food stamps to the hungry, and universities offer career training. These institutions allow Western individuals to access resources apart from patronage networks.

Patronage becomes essential when such formal institutions are weak—or absent. When state bureaucracies do not provide safety and services, people must know someone of influence to get what they need. To survive in a world marked by inequality and weak institutions, they need a patron to cover their backs. The best hope of security and stability is not in legal protections but in powerful patrons who can bend others to their will. Attaching oneself to a patron is the most realistic way to survive and move ahead in life. Poorer citizens do not seek patrons because they are lazy or incompetent, but because patronage is a strategic necessity in their context. Clients feel vulnerable, so they seek pragmatic alliances for covering. In contexts marked by inequality and weak institutions, people access resources through a network of patronage relationships.

## CONCLUSION

This chapter has explained the meaning and nuances of patronage. This provides a set of "hermeneutical glasses" to better interpret situations shaped by patronage.

Patronage is not like a board game with an official rulebook containing step-by-step instructions for the player.[19] Instead, people in Majority World contexts intuitively know how to function in "reciprocal relationships among unequals." For most people in the world, patron-client relationships are not theoretical but the natural way that relationships function in everyday life. Patronage is the air people breathe. Consequently, patronage permeates relationships throughout society, as the next chapter explores.

---

[19]David Maranz, *African Friends and Money Matters* (Dallas: SIL International, 2001), chapter 5.

# 2

# EXPRESSIONS OF PATRONAGE

IN MANY CULTURES, patronage is the modus operandi for relationships.[1] The Roman philosopher Seneca exalted benefaction as the "sacred bond" of shared humanity (cf. *Ben* 18.5; 19.9). The ideology of patronage is a ubiquitous framework that structures most relationships. Patronage is the grammar that people tacitly assume for social interactions.

Patronage is a default system that shapes many types of relationships, like a golden thread woven through society. As a result, patronage lends itself to many variations.[2] Some examples of patron-client relationships include parent-child, saint-devotee, ancestor-descendant, godparent-godchild, government-citizen, lord-vassal, landlord-tenant, politician-voter, general-soldier, donor-recipient, teacher-student, and host-guest. To illustrate concrete expressions of patronage, this chapter describes three of these common patronage relationships. Then we examine a story about Jesus, with several layers of patronage.

## GOVERNMENT AND CITIZENS

I grew up in a conservative community in rural America. So I learned the usual stereotypes about the Soviet Union—a godless nation where people had no freedoms and waited for hours to get bread. Then in 2002 I moved to a post-Soviet country in Central Asia. When I asked locals about their lives during the former Soviet Union era, they shared a different narrative:

---

[1]David E. Maranz, *African Friends and Money Matters* (Dallas, TX: SIL International, 2001); David deSilva, *Honor, Patronage, Kinship & Purity: Unlocking New Testament Culture* (Downers Grove, IL: IVP Academic, 2000), 119.
[2]Frederick W. Danker, *Benefactor: Epigraphic Study of a Greco-Roman and New Testament Semantic Field* (St. Louis, MO: Clayton Publishing House, 1982), 27.

the Soviets provided education, built factories, and constructed homes; everybody had a decent job and stable life. Central Asians themselves *loved* the Soviet Union and wished it would return!

When I asked people about the lack of personal freedoms and individual rights during the Soviet era, they responded, "Yeah, but the Soviets provided for us. I studied in Europe and traveled the world with the Red Army. Now I drive a taxi all day just to feed my family. How is this better?" Central Asians did not prioritize a democratic government. Rather, they would willingly sacrifice personal freedoms for security and prosperity. This explains the positive memories of the Soviet Union. The central government functioned as a patron: we'll take care of you in exchange for your loyalty. Many citizens gladly accepted this arrangement.

Patronage is the implicit social contract between many governments and their citizens. The legitimacy of authoritarian governments comes from their ability to provide goods for their citizens. Prime examples of governmental patronage include the Communist Party in China, the Saud family in Saudi Arabia, Hugo Chavez (d. 2013) in Venezuela, Vladimir Putin in Russia, and ancient Roman Caesars.[3] The president is the top patron who dispenses resources to retain political power. Their mandate to govern is not from elections, so they effectively purchase their right to govern with benevolence like public housing, free utilities, and economic growth. This notion of patronage also explains political leadership in Africa:

> Traditionally, [African] chiefs lived at the economic level of their fellow citizens because they gave away their wealth as fast as it came to them. They had high social position, but economically were on the level only a little above that of their subjects. . . . Present-day leaders in Africa who are unable or unwilling to distribute economic benefits to their followers have difficulties in maintaining their leadership and authority and retaining their followers.[4]

---

[3]Regarding patronage in Roman politics: "As a primary patron, the emperor gathered around him a select group of friends (*amici Caesaris*), whom he met on a personal basis at morning audiences (*salutations*) and banquets (*convivial*). They were the beneficiaries of imperial largesse in the form of offices, honors, and material gifts. In return, the emperor received the loyalty of an influential group of citizens. Despite their awesome power, Roman emperors lived in constant fear of conspiracies and rebellion. Patronal resources were deployed as a tool for maintenance of political power." Quoted from Raymond Westbrook, "Patronage in the Ancient Near East," *JESHO* 48, no. 2 (2005): 220-21.

[4]Maranz, *African Friends*, 8.

The social contract of patronage is rather simple: leaders provide and citizens follow. In this framework, leaders interpret dissent as a personal affront on their honor as patrons, so they retaliate harshly to preserve face. The liberal values of free speech and individual rights play second fiddle to the leader's public reputation.[5]

## HOST AND GUEST

In 2015 Abdul Dostum, an accused warlord from northern Afghanistan, became Afghanistan's vice president.[6] His political style mingles hospitality and patronage to maintain power. The *New York Times* article about Dostum's leadership style, entitled "Full Bellies Are the Measure of Afghan Influence and Hospitality," opens with this cultural description:

> It is an unassailable truth of Afghan politics, particularly after the advent of a democratic system here, that influence is gained one stomach at a time. Election gatherings, rallies and protests barely attract crowds if there is no promise of huge platters with small mountains of pilaf on them, the oilier the better. Politicians may break their campaign promises, but at least their supporters get fed.

Dostum leverages hospitality on a massive scale. Every day he feeds over one thousand guests in his sprawling palace. The full-time chef cooks hundreds of pounds of rice pilaf in huge tin pots. His militia guards and commanders feast alongside the local population. This hospitality requires several guesthouses and kitchens across his provinces in northern Afghanistan. Dostum boasts that he spends over $400,000 daily to feed guests. In the end, his generous hospitality procures tremendous loyalty. His soldiers wear his picture on their sleeve and his loyal electorate made him the country's second-ranking official.

---

[5]Diana Butler Bass explains how US President Donald Trump also adopts many aspects of this leadership style in her op-ed article "Thank Trump, or You'll Be Sorry," *The New York Times*, April 22, 2018, www.nytimes.com/2018/04/22/opinion/donald-trump-gratitude.html.

[6]This story and all quotes are cited from Mujib Mashal, "Full Bellies Are the Measure of Afghan Influence and Hospitality," *The New York Times*, August 23, 2015, www.nytimes.com/2015/08/24/world/asia/afghanistan-abdul-rashid-dostum-jowzjan-taliban.html. For further background, see Matthew Rosenberg, "Afghanistan's Vice President Is Barred from Entering U.S.," *The New York Times*, April 25, 2016, www.nytimes.com/2016/04/26/world/middleeast/abdul-rashid-dostum-afghanistan-barred-from-entering-us.html.

In 2001 Dostum's militia allegedly tortured and killed several hundred Taliban soldiers. When Dostum discussed these allegations with reporters, he felt slighted by the insult to his reputation as a generous host—"They gained weight here, I put them up in nice rooms, I fed them bananas, I fed them oranges. But they said, 'Dostum did this to me, Dostum did that.'"

The politics of Dostum reveal a key aspect about hospitality: the relationship between hosts and guests is one type of patronage. The grand scale of Dostum's hospitality is certainly unique. However, the same dynamics are present when one invites a neighbor for tea or visits a friend for dinner. In fact, hospitality may be the most common expression of patronage. Hospitality creates a sense of asymmetry between peers. In many countries, the host is the patron who regales guests, regardless of the financial costs. They cover the table with plates, insist that their guests eat more, and send guests home with more food—all displays of generosity. The guest is the client who receives food with thankfulness and speaks highly of the event. In these ways, the guest-host relationship functions according to the grammar of patronage.

## DONOR AND RECIPIENT

Galileo (1564–1642) was an Italian scientist, mathematician, and inventor. His observational experiments initiated the Scientific Revolution and earned him the title "father of science." But even with a brilliant mind, Galileo's scientific success depended upon patronage, a defining characteristic of Florentine society in Galileo's day. Before the days of universities, academics and scientists could not earn a living as professors. So intellectuals like Galileo had to work under the patronage of wealthy people to conduct and publish research. In the system of patron-backed science, the status of one's patron conferred scientific credibility. Artists and academics who worked under prominent patrons got more recognition. Patrons in turn gained honor from the arrangement. The religious and financial elite competed for notable clients as a way to enhance their status. Financing accomplished clients to perform research or produce artwork brought renown to their name.[7]

---

[7] This paragraph draws from Rice University, "A Brief History of Patronage," August 22, 2016, galileo .rice.edu/lib/student_work/florence96/jessdave/patronage.html.

Despite Galileo's many scientific accomplishments, he failed socially as a client. His advocacy of Copernicus's heliocentric astronomy implied that the Earth, and thereby the Catholic pope, was *not* the center of the universe. (No patron, however spiritual, welcomes that message.) Then in his written defense, Galileo publicly ridiculed the Pope as a simpleton. This alienated the Pope, who supported his research, and led to his house arrest until his death in 1642. Galileo ignored the most basic obligation of clients: honor thy patron.

In contemporary times, people who work in nonprofit sectors (e.g., the arts, education, research, social work) require funding from donors. For example, in the enterprise of Western missions, the supporter-missionary relationship is an example of patronage. Supporters give money on a regular basis, and the missionary recipient repays with visits, update letters, and token gifts from the host culture. This support-based model funds most Western missionary work.[8]

## JESUS AND THE CENTURION

The encounter between Jesus and the centurion in Luke 7:1-10 portrays an intricate web of patron-client relationships. First-century readers lived in a patronage culture, so they would have intuitively caught the nuances of patronage in this narrative. But modern readers, as cultural outsiders, might overlook these unmentioned social dynamics. So we analyze this story as a case study of about patron-client relationships.[9]

---

[8]Paul DeNeui, "Speaking of the Unspeakable: Money and Missions in Patron-Client Buddhist Cultures," in *Complexities of Money and Mission in Asia*, ed. Paul DeNeui (Pasadena, CA: William Carey Library, 2012), 110, has forthright insights on this matter.

It is not uncommon, however, for those same missionaries to have convinced themselves that their churches and financial givers back home are something entirely different from what Asians are seeking when they look for a supportive patron or ask for a small loan. Missionaries feel they have "raised their own support," whereas when a national asks for money for a particular need it is perceived as begging and lack of careful planning. The Western missionary views the relationship with her or his supporters as task-oriented and not necessarily personal in nature.

[9]For similar readings of this passage, see Halvor Moxnes, "Patron-Client Relations and the New Community in Luke-Acts," in *The Social World of Luke-Acts: Models for Interpretation*, ed. Jerome H. Neyrey (Grand Rapids: Baker Academic, 1999), 252-53; David deSilva, *Honor, Patronage, Kinship & Purity* (Downers Grove, IL: IVP Academic, 2000), 123-24.

> After Jesus had finished all his sayings in the hearing of the people, he entered Capernaum. A centurion there had a slave whom he valued highly, and who was ill and close to death. When he heard about Jesus, he sent some Jewish elders to him, asking him to come and heal his slave. When they came to Jesus, they appealed to him earnestly, saying, "He is worthy of having you do this for him, for he loves our people, and it is he who built our synagogue for us." And Jesus went with them, but when he was not far from the house, the centurion sent friends to say to him, "Lord, do not trouble yourself, for I am not worthy to have you come under my roof; therefore I did not presume to come to you. But only speak the word, and let my servant be healed. For I also am a man set under authority, with soldiers under me; and I say to one, 'Go,' and he goes, and to another, 'Come,' and he comes, and to my slave, 'Do this,' and the slave does it." When Jesus heard this he was amazed at him, and turning to the crowd that followed him, he said, "I tell you, not even in Israel have I found such faith." When those who had been sent returned to the house, they found the slave in good health. (Luke 7:1-10)

The centurion governed the area of Capernaum with a unit of one hundred soldiers. He maintained Roman rule in the Jewish town with a series of carrots (giving favors) and sticks (punishing dissent). The centurion derived power and resources from Rome, so was expected to maintain control for the emperor. He functionally brokered the patron-client relationship between Rome and this Judean community.

One day the centurion's slave becomes sick and needs medical attention. Luke says the centurion considered his servant to be "highly valued" (Gr. *entimos*, "upright" or "honorable"). In the first-century world where medical insurance did not cover healthcare expenses, the centurion assumes responsibility for this loyal worker. Like a good patron, the centurion leverages his network of relationships to solve the problem.

News of Jesus' healing miracles had spread throughout the region. The centurion wants to ask Jesus for help, but a direct appeal would not be appropriate, especially for an outsider, let alone a Gentile overlord. Dispatching mediators respects the power distance and rightly acknowledges Jesus' stature. So the centurion asks the local Jewish elders to make the connection on his behalf.

The centurion could request this favor from Jewish elders because he built a synagogue for them. Public buildings were a common form of benefaction in the Roman Empire. Buildings projected power, accumulated social capital, and ensured loyalty. The building indebted the Jewish leaders to the centurion, to whom they now owed a favor. So upon the centurion's request, the Jewish elders grant him access to their network of relationships and ask a favor on his behalf.

When appealing to Jesus, the Jews vouch for the centurion with patron-client rationale: "He is worthy of having you do this for him, for he loves our people, and it is he who built our synagogue for us." The centurion's virtuous benefaction makes him "worthy" of Jesus' help. By initiating the connection and esteeming the centurion's name, the elders are repaying their social obligations by brokering access to Jesus for the centurion.

Jesus hears their request and walks toward the centurion's house. But before Jesus arrives, the centurion sends his "friends" to mediate. In the ancient world, this term *friend* carried a different connotation than Western culture. A friend was not a buddy or golf partner, but an ally—someone you could trust to support your social standing. Such friendship was not based on emotional intimacy, but political reciprocity.[10] The Roman centurion depended upon his trustworthy friends to secure his interests. In Luke 7, the centurion's friends were political associates sent to facilitate the relationship with Jesus.

The friends' main objective is to secure Jesus' benefaction on behalf of the centurion. To accomplish this, they communicate honor to Jesus by giving deference, granting face, and affirming his status. Instead of waiting for Jesus to arrive, they approach him—a client's gesture of respectful deference. The first word of the encounter, "Lord," is an honorific title affirming Jesus' relational superiority. The mediators make a series of polite requests to avoid being presumptuous. This interaction is a positive honor exchange, "in which the powerful centurion, a powerful patron in the area, concedes larger honor to Jesus and addresses him as benefactor and patron."[11]

---

[10]According to Dio Chrysostom *Or.* 3:131-32, rulers granted political offices and military honors to buy "friends" as "means to forestall every possible rival." This picture of "friends" is found in Aristotle, *Nicomachean Ethics*, book 8; Cicero, *On Friendship*; Dio Chrysostom, *Orations 3*. Also, cf. John 19:12.

[11]Moxnes, "Patron-Client Relations," 253.

While showing deference to Jesus, the centurion also confirms his own status as a patron. The centurion has the authority to control people with mere words—"go," "come," "do this." His connection with Rome and leadership over soldiers means the centurion is prominent. But despite being a patron himself, the centurion is at the mercy of Jesus to acquire healing for his servant, and he trusts that Jesus can provide such a favor.

This story in Luke 7:1-10 involves many cultural aspects of patronage, as noted above. Three broader observations about this passage are worth noting. First, the words *patron, patronage,* or *client* are never mentioned. The reality of patronage was an unstated assumption guiding social interactions. The ideology of patronage implicitly shaped relationships at every level, as is often the case in patronage cultures.

Second, this short story illustrates the complexity of patronage. The six characters form a web of reciprocal exchanges. Patronage is communal, not bilateral. Moreover, the practice of patronage is fluid and adaptive, not static. In most relationships the centurion functions as the patron, but when a need arises, he seamlessly "steps down" to become a client in his relationship to Jesus. This transition between roles, depending on the relational context, was natural and normal.

Third, Jesus does not resist or reject the role of patron. Jesus walks into the system and uses it for kingdom purposes. In the end, Jesus is amazed by the centurion's faith and restores his slave's health. The centurion's appeal for Jesus' patronage was effective.

## CONCLUSION

Patronage influences a broad range of social interactions. These case studies from the Soviet Union, General Dostum, Galileo, and Jesus' healing are diverse examples of unequal, reciprocal relationships. Patron-client relationships are a pervasive and acceptable part of life in most cultures. However, not *all* cultures accept patronage as normal. Westerners look upon patronage with suspicion, and this leads to a cultural clash.

# 3

# MISPERCEPTIONS
# OF PATRONAGE

THE FAR SIDE OF OUR APARTMENT BUILDING in Central Asia had a dirt lot where homeless people often loitered. One day I left our apartment to go meet a friend. When I turned the corner towards the dirt lot, a homeless man got my attention. He claimed to be sick and asked for money to buy medicine. The city's main pharmacy was nearby, so I offered to buy the medicine he needed. Then he said the medicine was actually for his mother, so he preferred cash. As I asked questions, his story changed again and again.

At that moment, a torrent of anger swelled up within me. I felt so dirty and used. Even to this day, I remember the disgust I felt because of his request for money. I walked away surprised by my reaction. "Where did those emotions came from?" I asked myself. The man's request, though deceptive, was certainly understandable—he was a homeless guy who just wanted a few dollars. But his request for money somehow made me feel used and dehumanized.

This incident occurred in my second year of living in Central Asia, long before I learned anything about patronage. For two years I had given "loans" to local friends, but few of them repaid the money. According to my cultural interpretation, these people were stealing my money! I never confronted them about the unpaid loans, but my frustration accumulated. Then a single request for a few dollars unleashed a torrent of rage. Looking back, I believe my negative feelings were largely the result of a culture clash. Financial requests caused emotional angst because I interpreted those situations through my Western values, not the framework of patronage.

Complete this sentence with your own word(s): *When people ask me for money, I feel _____.*

Were your words negative or positive? Did the mere question evoke certain emotions or specific memories? Patronage is not just a topic of cultural study but something that touches our core values and relational identity. So to develop a healthy perspective of patronage, Westerners must be aware of their affective judgments and cognitive biases related to patronage.

This chapter explains how Westerners view patronage and why there is this cultural clash. This equips readers to process cultural interactions more accurately—without growing frustrated by patron-client relationships.

## THE WESTERN PERCEPTION

Ibaglo was a young Christian man who decided to attend college in the neighboring country of Cameroon. Before he left home, Ibaglo's pastor told him about Dale, a Western missionary in Cameroon. "When you arrive in Cameroon," said his African pastor, "be sure to find Dale. He will help you." For a young man seeking a university education, Ibaglo had high expectations of the relationship before they even met—Dale would be his patron and pay for his education. But for Dale, these expectations spoiled the relationship from the very outset.

Wycliffe missionary David Maranz explains, "Africans are flattered when they are asked to provide help. This gives them a sense of being useful, of thinking people have need of them. They are honored."[1] Ibaglo assumed Dale would feel honored to be a patron. But instead, the financial request annoyed and irritated Dale. He did not feel honored, and relationship never developed.

Westerners keep money out of their friendships. When money becomes a part of their relationships, people question motives or feel like a burden. Banks provide money, and friends provide fun (and certainly not vice

---

[1]David E. Maranz, *African Friends and Money Matters: Observations from Africa* (Dallas, TX: SIL International, 2001), 129. Paul DeNeui says, "In the Buddhist world of patron-client relationships, to be asked is to be honored" in his "Speaking of the Unspeakable: Money and Missions in Patron-Client Buddhist Cultures," in *Complexities of Money and Mission in Asia*, ed. Paul DeNeui (Pasadena, CA: William Carey Library, 2012), 110.

versa!). But patronage is a "financial friendship"—an oxymoron for Westerners who separate money and relationships. I've heard Westerners say, "They just want money, not a relationship." This comment reveals a deepseated cultural assumption: money and relationships should not mingle. The expectations of patronage seem morally wrong to Westerners. David deSilva opens his explanation of patronage with this observation:

> People in the United States and northern Europe may be culturally conditioned to find the concept of patronage distasteful at first and not at all a suitable metaphor for talking about God's relationship with us. When we say "it's not what you know but who you know," it is usually because we sense someone has an unfair advantage over us or over the friend whom we console with these words. It violates our conviction that everyone should have equal access to employment opportunities (being evaluated on the basis of pertinent skills rather than personal connection) or to services offered by private businesses or civic agencies.[2]

Westerners' distaste for patronage can lead to unhealthy views of people who request money. Clients seem like opportunists or manipulators. They are dismissed as dependents or sycophants who leach time and resources. Paul DeNeui explains, "Needing a patron may seem to some Westerners like the pitiful bird that cannot yet fly on its own strength. If the local person would simply plan ahead, set some money aside, and save instead of spending everything, they would not have to 'demean' themselves by 'begging.' Thus thinks the Westerner."[3] A client's constant need for help is a sign of immaturity to Westerners.

Westerners experience frustration with patronage at the personal level but are also critical of structural patronage in politics and economics. For Westerners, acquiring goods through relationships instead of official channels seems like corruption. We accuse leaders who offer positions to relatives of nepotism. Some even characterize patronage as organized crime.[4] This general perception is rather negative.

---

[2]David deSilva, *Honor, Patronage, Kinship, and Purity* (Downers Grove, IL: IVP Academic, 2000), 95.
[3]DeNeui, "Speaking of the Unspeakable," 108.
[4]E. Gellner, "Patrons and Clients," in *Patrons and Clients in Mediterranean Societies*, ed. E. Gellner and J. Waterbury (London: Duckworth, 1977). I would agree that organized crime involves patron-client relationships; but defining patronage *as* organized crime is an incorrect denunciation.

Influential publications, both Christian and secular, echo this negative view of patronage. In 2007 the Lausanne Committee for World Evangelization commissioned a survey of missions literature about money and international partnerships. The Lausanne report states that most missiological writings "see patron-client as a childish kind of relationship that we should all grow out of."[5] Western missiology characterizes patronage as juvenile and immature.

Francis Fukuyama is a prominent American political scientist and Senior Fellow at Stanford University. He offered this critical depiction of patronage:

> Feckless authoritarians must themselves adopt the language of democratic transition to legitimate their rule, even if in reality that power rests on patronage, kinship, ethnicity, or other narrow principles. . . . Bad governance, weak institutions, political corruption, and patronage exist because certain powerful political actors have a strong self-interest in the status quo.[6]

Notice the pejorative associations with patronage—feckless authoritarians, narrow principles, bad governance, political corruption, and strong self-interest. This is a moral indictment, not a neutral description. Fukuyama's denunciation illustrates Western antipathy towards patronage. So then, why does Western culture have a pejorative view of patronage?

## CULTURAL DIFFERENCES

Fundamental cultural differences between patronage and Western economics make the cultural clash inevitable. Think of each cultural system as a rulebook for playing a board game. Each player assumes others will "play by the rules." But once the game starts, it becomes evident the players have different, even contradicting, rulebooks. This metaphor explains the nature of cultural tensions—cultures assume differing "rules" for how life *should* function. To get at the root of the cultural tensions, this section contrasts seven key differences between the cultural rulebooks of Western and

---

[5]Global Mapping International, "Oxford Initiative: Phase 1, Literature Survey," (2008), 6. This comment was made during the review of the exception to this tendency, the publications of Delbert Chinchen.
[6]Francis Fukuyama, *America at the Crossroads: Democracy, Power, and the Neoconservative Legacy* (New Haven, CT: Yale University Press, 2007), 130, 148.

Majority World socioeconomic systems (see table 3.1). Remember, these seven contrasts describe the end points of a broad continuum. They are general social patterns, not absolute rules.

|  | WESTERN WORLD | MAJORITY WORLD |
|---|---|---|
| Primary System | Bureaucracy | Patronage |
| Natural Logic | Rules define relationships | Relationships define rules |
| Key Value | Integrity | Harmony |
| Nature of Money | Private | Public |
| Financial Objective | Independency | Mutuality |
| Source of Income | Ability | Family |
| Expectation | Fairness | Favoritism |
| Exchange of Gifts | Charity | Reciprocity |

**Table 3.1.** Basic cultural differences

***Rules vs. relationships.*** Since the Enlightenment, Western cultures have assumed reality is governed by rules. Scientists discover and master the rules operating the stars, the human body, and even the economy. This mechanistic view of reality also assumes that "rules define relationships." This means laws, whether divine or municipal, should govern society. Rules always apply to all people at all times, no exceptions. The rules trump relational considerations.[7]

In Majority World cultures the converse is true—"relationships define rules." Traditional cultures (like those of the Bible) do in fact have rules, but "they merely describe the visible working of an underlying relationship, which was the truly defining element."[8] Rules are generic guidelines, which means exceptions are easily made to preserve relationships. "A good patron is someone who has sufficient influence to intercede on behalf of the weak client and provide an 'exemption' from some decision through influencing a decision-maker."[9] In the system of patronage, people are expected to act according to relational

---

[7]E. Randolph Richards and Brandon J. O'Brien, *Misreading Scripture with Western Eyes: Removing Cultural Blinders to Better Understand the Bible* (Downers Grove, IL: IVP Books, 2012), 157-75, explain these cultural patterns in a chapter about patronage, titled "First Things First: Rules and Relationships."
[8]Richards and O'Brien, *Misreading Scripture*, 159.
[9]Perry Shaw, "Patronage, Exemption, and Institutional Policy," *EMQ* 49:1 (Jan 2013): 9.

obligations. The social context determines which rules apply. The Western emphasis on "the rule of law" comes across as relationally cold and heartless.

***Integrity vs. harmony.*** To say a person has integrity is a high compliment for Westerners, especially in financial matters. This means the person is uncorrupted and has strong moral principles. They follow the rules and are unaffected by relationships. But in patronage cultures, relational harmony is the central value. People make decisions to stay relationally connected, especially to their patrons. Cultures of patronage do value integrity, but their sense of integrity means keeping relational obligations, not official rules.

***Private vs. public.*** "How much money do you make?" This question rankles many Westerners who live abroad. In Western cultures finances are private. Money is for personal use and should not be discussed. Not even my own mother or brother knows my salary, nor would they ask! Americans discuss many personal issues, but personal wealth is not one of them.

For cultures in Asia or Africa, money is public. The wealthy publicize their riches, verbally and symbolically, so that people know their status and grant them proper respect. Recall how the Afghan politician Dostum (chapter two) boasted about spending $400,000 per day to feed people. Patrons broadcast their wealth and generosity to enhance their honor. In such a context, inquiring about a person's salary fulfills several functions. At one level, the question is lobbing a proverbial softball for the wealthy person to claim a grand status. Also, the answer lets the inquirer know whether a person is a potential patron. These dynamics are the reason why money is a public issue.

***Independence vs. mutuality.*** Americans love freedom. Banks offer financial freedom; God gives emotional freedom; soldiers guard national freedom; the constitution ensures personal freedoms. Let freedom ring! Freedom means independence, not needing other people. In Western cultures, being dependent is a severe character flaw. So parents aim to raise independent children.

The system of patronage however is based on mutual interdependence. Clients need patrons to help them. This is not a vice but a reality of the economic circumstances. Patronage relationships allow for dependence, but that is not their defining feature. The aim of patronage is mutuality; patrons and clients depend upon each other. People want to be in an interdependent network. Seeking relational independence is social suicide. Here again, the primary objectives of each system, independence and mutuality, stand in opposition.

*Ability vs. family.* In Central Asia, I helped operate a small café. The manager of the café, Orgon, was a national believer and close friend. The café had to hire a new administrator to purchase groceries and track finances. Orgon and I sat down to discuss our options for the new hire. I listed the key qualifications for the job. When I finished, Orgon said that he wanted to hire his younger brother for the job. Everything within me was thinking, "Wait, you can't do that! Sure, I want to help your family, but that is nepotism!" But for Orgon the choice was perfectly logical—he could trust his brother to be loyal and not steal money. Moreover, Orgon expected to use his managerial position to help his brother. As the oldest son, Orgon would betray his family if he did *not* hire his brother.

Later, when I was in America, I retold this incident to a police officer who worked for the Los Angeles Police Department. He noted that could *never* happen at the LAPD. The hiring process involves multiple layers of bureaucracy to avoid any possible conflict of interest and ensure people are hired solely on merit.

These two hiring processes illustrate opposing cultural values. In the West, financial opportunities are based on ability, defined by one's work experience and education. In the system of patronage, money comes from your relatives. Businesses are family-operated, and income is shared with all the relatives. Hiring a nonrelative seems bizarre, if not dumb: Why would you give away your money to a stranger?

*Fairness vs. favoritism.* Should resources be distributed according to fairness or favoritism? Political systems in the West are

> a universalist society with a central government and bureaucracy. In this type of society, citizens expect to have access on an equal basis to goods and services provided by the state. . . . Thus, these goods and services are regarded as a right, not as a favor provided by the state.[10]

---

[10]Halvor Moxnes, "Patron-Client Relations and the New Community in Luke-Acts," in *The Social World of Luke-Acts: Models for Interpretation*, ed. Jerome H. Neyrey (Peabody, MA: Hendrickson, 1991), 243.

Fairness means equal access for everyone, regardless of circumstances.

But in patronage, you are supposed to give favors to people whom you can surely trust—your favorites. Giving preference to your own people preserves your place in the community. A wealthy person must share resources with people they know. To not play favorites would be a shameful misuse of your influence.

***Charity vs. reciprocity.*** In contexts of patronage, gifts cement relationships. Gifts express a social bond and recognize a person's worth. So, to maintain relationships, reciprocity and obligation are essential in gift-giving. A gift confers a benefit that elicits some reciprocal return to continue the relationship.[11] Gifts create and enhance relational bonds. Clients who receive gifts are under a strong, albeit non-legal, obligation to reciprocate in some way. In other words, gifts come with strings attached.

Gifts in Western contexts carry a very different meaning. They are given gratuitously, without obligation or expectation of repayment. Any expectation of a return stains the gift and the motive of the giver. Westerners see gifts as a one-way exchange, with *no* strings attached. So, for example, they give charitable contributions anonymously (lit. "without name"), meaning a return is not even possible. This concept of an unreciprocated "gift" is foreign in most cultures.

## CONCLUSION

Encounters with patronage cause stressful emotions, relational strains, and negative judgments for Westerners. The core values of Majority World and Western economic systems often clash in key areas. So we should expect tensions when these cultural systems intersect. The culture clash triggers emotional frustration, which then reinforces the negative viewpoint of patronage. Understanding the differences between the two cultural systems can mitigate (not eliminate) the cultural tensions.

Up to this point, I have sought to *explain* patronage. However, we must also *evaluate* patronage. Is it good, or bad? How should we as Christians engage patronage? To answer these questions, the next three chapters explore patronage in the Bible.

---

[11]John M. G. Barclay, *Paul and the Gift* (Grand Rapids: Eerdmans, 2015), 575. Also, pages 57-63 provide a helpful explanation of social gifting.

PART TWO

# BIBLICAL MODELS

# 4

# YAHWEH AND ISRAEL

THE TASK OF DEVELOPING A BIBLICAL THEOLOGY of patronage faces an obvious challenge: the language of patronage is rather scant in the Bible. The words *patron*, *client*, and *patronage* never appear in the Bible, and *benefactor* is used only twice (Luke 22:25; Romans 16:2). Synthesizing verses with the key terms will not produce a biblical theology of patronage.

However, patronage does appear prominently throughout the Bible as an assumed framework. Patronage was the de facto socioeconomic model for relationships in biblical cultures, a central feature of their worldview. Therefore, the model of patronage remains "an appropriate framework for interpreting the patterned social relations that are observable in the biblical literature."[1] Like most cultural values, patronage is assumed, not stated. For this reason, biblical writers need not use the terminology of "patron/age" to allude to the concept. So our methodology for developing a biblical theology of patronage is to ask descriptive questions: How did biblical figures engage patronage? How did people in the Bible utilize the framework of patronage to develop relationships and express truth(s)? How did salvation-history take shape in contexts of patronage?

The next three chapters look at the examples of Yahweh (Old Testament), Jesus (Gospels), and Paul (epistles) to develop a biblical theology of patronage. These three biblical figures each adopted and transformed patronage relationships for kingdom purposes. Their examples of ministry in patron-client contexts (chapters 4–6) provide essential principles for theology (chapters 7–9) and ministry (chapters 10–12). Their examples present a model of patronage that is both God-centered and life-giving.

---

[1]Ronald Simkins, "Patronage and the Political Economy of Monarchic Israel," *Semeia* 87 (1999): 128.

## YAHWEH'S COVENANT RELATIONSHIP

The basis of Yahweh's relationship with Israel was a *covenant*—a relational agreement based on reciprocity.[2] According to Walter Eichrodt, this covenant-relationship between Yahweh and Israel was "the concept in which Israelite thought gave definitive expression."[3] The covenant is a central and unifying theme in Old Testament life and theology.

The covenant relationship meant fulfilling commitments and keeping promises. In the Old Testament covenant, Yahweh provided benefits such as salvation, shalom, and blessings. In response, Israel offered praise, thanks, and obedience to God. Yahweh is the patron who provides material favors; Israel is the client who repays with honor (see figure 4.1). Israel gets abundant life, and God gets the glory. The Yahweh-Israel covenant was a reciprocal relationship among unequals, i.e., patronage. In other words, "Patronage is the root metaphor underlying the fundamental idea of covenant in the biblical literature."[4]

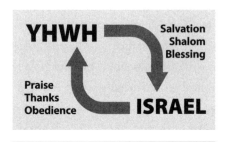

**Figure 4.1.** The Yahweh-Israel patronage relationship

## THE SINAI COVENANT AS SUZERAIN TREATY

International relations in the days of ancient Israel were often characterized by suzerainty. In this arrangement, the king of a powerful nation (i.e.,

---

[2]The covenant refers to both an initial agreement between two parties and the ongoing union.

[3]Walther Eichrodt, *Theology of the Old Testament*, trans. J. A. Baker (Philadelphia: Westminster John Knox, 1967) 1:36. Eichrodt contended covenant was *the* center of the Old Testament. However, many note a diversity of OT theologies and the absence of covenant in some Wisdom literature. Nevertheless, all agree the concept of covenant does structure Israel's worldview far beyond the limited occurrences of the Hebrew word *berit*.

[4]Simkins, "Patronage and the Political Economy," 129.

*suzerain*) controlled the affairs of weaker vassal states. In exchange for the suzerain's protection and coverage, the vassal paid tribute and deferred to the suzerain. The suzerain expected loyalty and allegiance from the vassal. This patronage relationship was formalized with a "suzerain-vassal treaty"— a covenant agreement between a superior and inferior. Archeologists have discovered hundreds of clay tablets with suzerain-vassal treaties in the ancient Near East (especially among the Hittite and Assyrian peoples).[5]

Interestingly, Yahweh used this same treaty format to define his relationship with Israel. Yahweh ratified a suzerain-vassal treaty with Israel to communicate the nature and expectations of their relationship. "Hittite vassal treaties established a patronage relationship between the local kings and the Hittite emperor, and the biblical covenant did the same between God and Israel."[6] The Mosaic Covenant in Exodus 19–24 follows the pattern of suzerain-vassal treaties, as table 4.1 outlines.[7]

| ELEMENTS OF SUZERAIN-VASSAL TREATY | MOSAIC COVENANT |
|---|---|
| 1. Preamble (identity of suzerain) | Exodus 20:2–"I am the LORD your God" |
| 2. History (past benevolence) | Exodus 20:2–"who brought you out of the land of Egypt" |
| 3. Stipulations (the vassal's obligations) | Exodus 20:4–23 :19–"you shall . . ." |
| 4. Deposit (a public reminder) | Exodus 24:4-8 –the blood of the covenant |
| 5. Blessings and curses (consequences of [dis]loyalty) | Exodus 23:20-33 –the promised conquest of Canaan |

**Table 4.1.** Suzerain-vassal treaties

The Ten Commandments and Sinai covenant "represent an agreement between a superior party (God) and a subordinate party (Israel). In return for past deliverance, and future provision, undivided loyalty in all manners is expected of Israel."[8] The Torah was not a legal contract in the modern sense but more like a marriage pledge between a kinsman-redeemer and a

---

[5]As the Amarna letters indicate, Egypt also maintained patron-client arrangements with vassal states in the Levant, but it was mostly implicit. They did not ratify the covenant with an official treaty document and/or oath at the same rate as the Hittites in central Anatolia.

[6]Raymond Westbrook, "Patronage in the Ancient Near East," *JESHO* 48, no. 2 (2005): 215.

[7]Paul R. House, *Old Testament Theology* (Downers Grove, IL: IVP Academic, 1998), 117. Other scholars reference Exodus 19, where the same elements are also found.

[8]J. W. Marshall, "Decalogue," in *Dictionary of the Old Testament: Pentateuch*, ed. T. Desmond Alexander and David W. Baker (Downers Grove, IL: IVP Academic, 2003), 174.

hopeless orphan (cf. Ezekiel 16:1-14). The creator God has benevolently rescued the nation of Israel, so they must express their submission and allegiance. The new relationship required covenantal faithfulness from Israel. Allegiance would bring blessings, and disloyalty would lead to curses and perhaps end the covenantal relationship (cf. Deuteronomy 27–28).[9] One might paraphrase the covenant preamble of Exodus 19:4-6 as such:

> You saw how I am stronger than the Egyptians, how I delivered and redeemed you from your shameful state. Now therefore you must reciprocate: if you give me your allegiance and remain loyal to the covenant, then you shall be my favored clients out of all peoples. I can make this happen as a trustworthy patron, because I am sovereign over everything.

The books of Exodus and Deuteronomy used the standard form of ancient Near Eastern treaties. The people of Israel thus interpreted the Sinai covenant (Exodus 19–24) as a suzerain-vassal treaty: God is the suzerain/patron, and Israel was the vassal/client. Yahweh deliberately chose the cultural form of suzerain-vassal treaty in order to form a patronage relationship with Israel.

### *HESED* AND LOVE: THE COVENANT BOND

Loyalty is the invisible bond that sustains patron-client relationships. The patron is loyal by fulfilling his promises and sustaining his people. One Hebrew word in particular embodies Yahweh's covenant loyalty and trustworthiness, *hesed*. Old Testament scholars bemoan the lack of English equivalents for *hesed*, which is often translated "lovingkindness," "steadfast love," or "mercy." *Hesed* denotes God's relational commitment or covenant loyalty, thus referring to the ideology of patronage. Scholars explain, "the term *hesed* in the Hebrew Bible is indicative of patronage"[10] and "articulates the very essence of patronage."[11] God manifested his *hesed* through covenant-keeping patronage (cf. Daniel 9:4) and demonstrable

---

[9]The language and logic of suzerain-vassal treaties saturate the entire Pentateuch. Deuteronomy is heavily based on such a treaty, both literarily and theologically.

[10]Westbrook, "Patronage in the Ancient Near East," 215.

[11]Niels Peter Lemche, "Kings and Clients: On Loyalty Between the Ruler and the Ruled in Ancient 'Israel,'" *Semeia* 66 (1994): 126.

faithfulness to the relationship. Psalms 117:2 says, "For great is his steadfast love [*hesed*] toward us, and the faithfulness of the LORD endures forever." Old Testament scholar Ronald Simkins explains, "Yahweh is the divine patron who protects and provides for his people Israel. Yahweh's loyalty to his people is expressed by *hesed*."[12] In short, the key Old Testament word *hesed* suggests the benefits of covenant, patronage, and benevolence.

Love was another vital feature of the patronage covenant (Deuteronomy 6:5; cf. Matthew 22:37). In ancient Mediterranean contexts, *love* referred not to platonic affections, but to the relational loyalty of a covenant partner.[13] "To 'hate' in a treaty context means to violate covenant; to 'love' means to conform to covenant stipulations."[14] Covenantal love was expressed through loyalty and service. The fact that God loves his client Israel means he faithfully keeps his promise and maintains *hesed*. Deuteronomy 7:8-9 explicitly connects love and covenant-keeping.

> It was because the LORD loved you and kept the oath that he swore to your ancestors, that the LORD brought you out with a mighty hand, and redeemed you from the house of slavery, from the hand of Pharaoh king of Egypt. Know therefore that the LORD your God is God, the faithful God who maintains covenant loyalty with those who love him and keep his commandments, to a thousand generations.

The language of *love* implies fidelity and trustworthiness—the covenantal expectations of patronage.[15]

## TEMPLE SACRIFICES: GIFTS FROM ISRAEL THE CLIENT

The Sinai covenant established an ongoing relationship in which God was the Patron and Israel was the client. Israel was obliged to honor God with

[12]Simkins, "Patronage and the Political Economy," 129.
[13]William L Moran, "Ancient Near Eastern Background of the Love of God in Deuteronomy," *CBQ* 25, no. 1 (January 1963): 77-87.
[14]Saul M. Olyan, "Honor, Shame, and Covenant Relations in Ancient Israel and Its Environment," *JBL* 115, no. 2 (1996): 210.
[15]This parallels Jonathan Edwards, who equates loving God with honoring God. Our love towards God, he says, "is expressed in a high esteem of God, admiration of his perfections, [delight] in them, and praise of them." Quoted from John Piper, *God's Passion for His Glory: Living the Vision of Jonathan Edwards* (Wheaton, IL: Crossway, 2006), 158.

obedience and allegiance, lest they break the covenant and experience shame. David deSilva explains,

> One of the basic ideological underpinnings of the [Sinai] covenant was that those who honored God by keeping the covenant stipulations would be honored by God, while those who showed contempt for God and his honor by neglecting or violating those stipulations would themselves be subjected to contempt and disgrace.[16]

Tragically, Israel was a disloyal covenant partner who failed to love their patron. They sought false gods for blessings and offered allegiance to pagan kings for protection. Israel repeatedly failed to trust in God alone for patronage and salvation. These actions dishonored Yahweh, their trustworthy provider. Malachi 1–2 is one example of how Israel failed to honor God as his clients—the priests offered disrespectful gifts to Yahweh.

In the opening lines of Malachi, God accuses the priesthood of dishonoring, disrespecting, and despising him. "'If then I am a father, where is the *honor* due me? And if I am a master, where is the *respect* due me? says the LORD of hosts to you, O priests, who *despise* my name" (Malachi 1:6, italics added). The priests have despised the Lord's table by sacrificing lame and sick animals. These defective sacrifices are not portrayed as transgressing a legal code but rather as not fulfilling the expectations of patron-client reciprocity. God compares their sacrifices to an inappropriate gift. "Try presenting that to your governor; will he be pleased with you or show you favor?" (Malachi 1:8). No sane Israelite would take a dirty, used gift to their governor when seeking a favor. Their social conscious, not to mention the threat of public humiliation, would not allow such a disgrace. Blemished gifts insult powerful patrons, yet the priests presented unsightly animals to the "great King" (Malachi 1:14). God felt so despised he tells the priests to close the temple doors and keep the animals to themselves (Malachi 1:10).

The priests' defective gifts defamed God, so he vindicates his name by dishonoring them. God tells the priests, "You have corrupted the covenant of Levi . . . and so I make you despised and abased before all the people"

---

[16]David deSilva, "Honor and Shame," in *Dictionary of the Old Testament: Pentateuch*, ed. T. Desmond Alexander and David W. Baker (Downers Grove, IL: IVP Academic, 2003), 435.

(Malachi 2:8-9 ESV). God would avenge the insults in a spectacular show of humiliation—"I will rebuke your offspring, and spread dung on your faces, the dung of your offerings, and I will put you out of my presence" (Malachi 2:3).

The priests' behavior in the days of Malachi stands in sharp contrast to Phinehas, the father of Israel's priesthood. In Numbers 25, to preserve national holiness, Phinehas kills the Israelites who were sleeping with Midianites. After that event, God says about Phinehas, "He and his descendants will have a covenant of a lasting priesthood, because he was zealous for the honor of his God and made atonement for the Israelites" (Numbers 25:13 NIV). Because Phineas placed God's honor above all else, God granted Phineas and his Levite descendants the sacred responsibility of mediating Israel's gifts to God.

The purpose of sacrifices was to honor God as the patron (cf. Malachi 1:6, 11; 2:2, 5). They were not repayment, "but a communication of the donor's desire for an ongoing relationship with the recipient, *namely patronage*."[17] The public offering of an animal demonstrated Israel's commitment and maintained covenant relations. The sacrifices communicated respect and deference to the patron. "Animal sacrifices provided atonement for unintentional affronts against God's honor (Leviticus 4:2-3; 5:5-6)."[18] Within the framework of patron-client reciprocity, sacrifices were gifts intended to honor and thank God.[19] This aspect of Israel's cultic life reflects a broader theological reality in the Old Testament: God expected Israel to be a loyal client who honored him.

## THE EXILE AND YAHWEH'S REPUTATION AS PATRON

Yahweh was the suzerain who protected and preserved Israel. The Sinai covenant obliged God to bless his people with military victory, abundant crops, and healthy families (Deuteronomy 6–7; cf. Genesis 12:1-3). In return, God would receive honor and glory as Israel's patron. Because

---

[17]Westbrook, "Patronage in the Ancient Near East," 220, emphasis added.
[18]deSilva, "Honor and Shame," 435.
[19]The OT sacrifices had other effects as well. The sacrificial system also ensured purity/holiness (Lev 14) and atoned for sin (Lev 19:22). Yet these functions are compatible with (not distinct from) sacrifice's ultimate function of gifting honor to God.

patronage structured Israel's relationship with Yahweh, instances of national disgrace threw into question Yahweh's trustworthiness. Israel's humiliation meant God abdicated his role as patron; he was not being faithful to his clients.

Psalm 74 laments a disaster that had befallen Israel—the temple was laid to ruin. Israel had been put to shame, and they accuse God of forgetting the covenant. But the main concern of Psalm 74 is not just Israel's own shame and suffering. God's failure to defend Israel makes *him* lose face. The enemies of Israel defile, revile, and mock God's name. The Psalmist mentions this deplorable fact five times (NIV, emphases added).

> They *defiled* the dwelling place of your Name. (Psalm 74:7)
> How long will the enemy *mock* you, God? (Psalm 74:10a)
> Will the foe *revile* your name forever? (Psalm 74:10b)
> Foolish people have *reviled* your name. (Psalm 74:18)
> Fools *mock* you all day long. (Psalm 74:22)

Israel's exile meant Yahweh was not being faithful to the glory of his own Name (cf. Isaiah 42:8). So Psalm 74 beseeches God to show concern for his reputation and to restore *his* honor.

> The cry for Yahweh to rise up and plead his cause operates as a demand from a disquieted client to his unresponsive patron. The psalmist knows that until the unresponsive patron acts, the roar of the adversaries will continue unabated (v. 23), and that both Yahweh and the community will continue to garner shame.[20]

The psalmist petitions God to rise up as a mighty patron (NIV, emphases added).

> *Remember* how the enemy has mocked you, Lord. (Psalm 74:18)
> *Have regard* for your covenant. (Psalm 74:20)
> *Do not let* the oppressed retreat in disgrace; may the poor and needy praise your name. (Psalm 74:21)
> *Rise up*, O God, and *defend* your cause; *remember* how fools mock you all day long. (Psalm 74:22)

---

[20]W. Dennis Tucker Jr., "Is Shame a Matter of Patronage in the Communal Laments?" *JSOT* 31, no. 4 (2007): 479.

Until Yahweh silences his adversaries and restores Israel, the patron and his clients will continue in shame. God is disgraced for not keeping his part of the reciprocal relationship. The lament of Psalm 74

> attempts to restore honor to the client-community [Israel] by recognizing the shame of the failed Patron [Yahweh]. The shamed Patron must act in a manner consistent with his reciprocal obligations to earn honor. Honor cannot be extended to the client-community until honor has been restored for the Patron.[21]

Earlier in Israel's history, Moses uses this same patronage logic to influence God's behavior. On day one of the new relationship, Israel violates the covenant; they make a golden calf. They praise this surrogate patron for past deliverance and trust it for future protection (Exodus 32:1-6). This idolatry ridicules God's benevolence (both past and future). Israel's ungratefulness insults their patron, who deserves glory. So God prepares to annihilate the unfaithful and disobedient people (Exodus 32:7-10). But Moses appeals to God's reputation as a patron by imploring him to consider how the Egyptians would gossip about him (Exodus 32:11-13). Moses reasons to God, if you harm us, then you might lose face as others will think shamefully of you. In the end, God accepts the logic of patronage from Moses: "The LORD changed his mind about the disaster" (Exodus 32:14). God played his part as patron and preserved the glory of his name.[22] Moses' blatant appeal to patronage saved Israel from divine judgment.

In times of national distress, Moses and the psalmists (cf. Psalms 44, 79, and 89) implored God to preserve his own honor by preserving his clients. This reflects a prominent feature of Old Testament theology, God as the faithful patron of Israel.

## BROKERS OF GOD'S PATRONAGE

While enthroned in the heavens, God selected earthly intermediaries to dispense his salvific blessings. God channeled his benevolence to Israel and

---

[21]Tucker, "Is Shame a Matter of Patronage," 475.

[22]Westbrook, "Patronage in the Ancient Near East," 217. An Old Babylonian letter in which a client reminds his patron of how unreliability diminishes prestige: "Do you not know that a gentleman whose household members cannot trust him loses face in his own palace and he himself is contemptible?"

humanity primarily through brokers: kings, prophets, and wisdom. Brokerage was another way God used patronage to accomplish his mission.

The Davidic covenant formed a patron-client relationship between Yahweh and David's family. In 2 Samuel 7:8-16 Yahweh "bestows kingship as a divine grant upon the house of David—a gift of gratitude from the patron for service or loyalty previously rendered by the client."[23] The preamble of this suzerain-vassal treaty recalls how God's benevolent grace exalted David from ignominy to prominence: "I took you from the pasture, from following the sheep to be the prince over my people Israel" (2 Samuel 7:8). God the patron has gifted many favors upon David: "I have been with you. . . . I will make for you a great name. . . . I will give you rest. . . . I will raise up your offspring. . . . I will establish the throne of his kingdom" (2 Samuel 7:9-13). God then makes a covenant promise to David, "Your house and your kingdom shall be made sure forever before me; your throne shall be established forever" (2 Samuel 7:16). God says about David's son, "I will be a father to him, and he shall be a son to me" (2 Samuel 7:14). The customary language of "father" and "son" confirms an intimate patron-client relationship (cf. 2 Kings 16:5-9). David, as a grateful client, praises God with exuberant thankfulness (2 Samuel 7:18-29). In this way, God forms a patron-client covenant with David's royal family.

David and his royal family were God's clients-kings who ruled over Israel.[24] The king's unique relationship with God equipped him with resources to distribute throughout the land. God exalted David as king to protect the people, ensure justice, and defend against the wicked. The king received and channeled God's blessings to the people, who in turn demonstrated their loyalty to the king (e.g., 2 Samuel 14:22). In sum, "patronage was the social structure of the political economy of monarchic Israel."[25] The Davidic monarchy brokered God's salvation to Israel.

Prophets were also brokers of divine salvation because of their direct access to God. A prophet could "use his influence to bestow benefits uniquely within divine power, such as birth of a child and revival of the

---

[23]Simkins, "Patronage and the Political Economy," 129.
[24]Lemche, "Kings and Clients," 126.
[25]Simkins, "Patronage and the Political Economy," 140.

dead."[26] In 1 Kings 17, Elijah provides the poor widow with a limitless supply of food. He becomes her patron, and so she reciprocates by feeding him from those provisions. When her son later dies, she accuses Elijah of failing to protect her from harm. Elijah's plea with God assumes her status as a client: "LORD my God, have you brought tragedy even on this widow I am staying with, by causing her son to die?" (1 Kings 17:20). Reviving the son confirms Elijah's identity as an intermediary of God: "Now I know that you are a man of God" (1 Kings 17:24).[27]

Divine wisdom was an impersonal broker who mediated God's blessings to the people of Israel. The book of Proverbs personifies wisdom as a moral agent who receives praise and obedience in exchange for the favors she bestows. "Cherish [wisdom], and she will exalt you; embrace her, and she will honor you. She will give you a garland to grace your head and present you with a glorious crown" (Proverbs 4:8-9). People who loyally obey her words will receive life and divine favor (Proverbs 8:32-36), so a proper relationship with her is vital (Proverbs 13:18).[28] Like kings and prophets, wisdom was a conduit of God's patronage blessings to humanity.

## CONCLUSION

Yahweh's relationship with Israel was a covenant of patronage. God assumed the role of suzerain who would provide land, blessing, and protection. Israel reciprocated with praise, thanks, and loyalty. As per God's design, patronage structured the covenantal relationship between Israel and Yahweh.

Patronage in the Old Testament reflected cultural patterns from Israel's neighbors yet was also radically countercultural. God transformed the system of patronage in key ways. Yahweh's form of patronage was uniquely *God-centered* and *life-giving*. The signature distinction of patronage in ancient Israel was the identity of the patron. Israel's patron was Yahweh—not

---

[26]Westbrook, "Patronage in the Ancient Near East," 230.

[27]Westbrook, "Patronage in the Ancient Near East," 228.

[28]Ancient Greco-Romans authors used the explicit language of benefaction to praise *sōfia* (i.e., philosophy/knowledge/wisdom). See Zeba A. Crook, *Reconceptualising Conversion: Patronage, Loyalty, and Conversion in the Religions of the Ancient Mediterranean* (New York: De Gruyter, 2004), 100-108. Though anachronistic for interpreting Proverbs, this illustrates that patronage could structure the wisdom-learner relationship in ancient cultures.

Egypt, Nebuchadnezzar, or Baal, nor any other kingdom, king, or deity. Biblical patronage is radically God-centered. Also, God's patronage brought abundant life to his clients. Ancient suzerains often treated clients like a golden goose to be squeezed for as much as possible. The king of Egypt and Assyria levied crippling tributes upon their vassals, and pagan gods demanded human life from their worshipers. In contrast, Yahweh's patronage brought blessings for his people. God bestowed life upon Israel (and through Israel, the whole world). These aspects of Yahweh's patronage—*God-centered* and *life-giving*—also characterize the ministries of Jesus and Paul, and become the main principles for contemporary ministry, as we shall further explore.

# 5

# JESUS AND THE KINGDOM

LIFE IN THE ROMAN EMPIRE during the time of Jesus revolved around
patronage. Patron-client relationships were so pervasive in Roman society
the philosopher Cicero believed "the origins of Roman *clientela* [i.e., pa-
tronage] were so ancient that it must have been brought to Rome by Ro-
mulus [the mythical city-founder] himself."[1] Rome without patronage was
inconceivable. Classics professor Jo-Ann Shelton says, "The patronage
system was one of the most deep-rooted and pervasive aspects of ancient
Roman society."[2] Roman patronage began at the top with Caesar's benevolent distributions to loyal citizens and touched every sphere of society. The
vast majority of people in the Roman Empire were impoverished, making
patronage an essential survival strategy for the vulnerable who faced
grinding poverty.[3]

Jesus and the apostles ministered in this Greco-Roman society shaped
by patronage. They could not have avoided the dynamics of patron-client
relationships. In line with the previous chapter, we use a descriptive approach to discern Jesus' view of patronage: How did he engage and
transform patronage for kingdom purposes in his ministry? First, we
examine how Jesus himself played the role of patron; then, what Jesus
taught about patronage.

---

[1]Mario Biagioli, *Galileo, Courtier: The Practice of Science in the Culture of Absolutism* (Chicago: University of Chicago Press, 1993), 15.

[2]Jo-Ann Shelton, *As the Romans Did: A Source Book in Roman Social History* (New York: Oxford University Press, 1988), 14.

[3]Historical research indicates that 99 percent of the population never fully escaped poverty. Nearly
70 percent lived at a subsistence level, meaning they were one incident away from ruin. See Verlyn
Verbrugge and Keith R. Krell, *Paul and Money: A Biblical and Theological Analysis of the Apostle's Teachings and Practices* (Grand Rapids: Zondervan, 2015), 108-10.

## THE PATRONAGE OF JESUS

Jesus proclaimed and mediated the good news of God's favor in every aspect of his ministry. His healings on behalf of the demonized and sick were benefactions to those in need. Peter said that Jesus "went about benefacting and healing" (Acts 10:38, author's translation).[4] Within the ideology of patronage, Jesus' miraculous provisions of bread to the hungry (cf. Matthew 14; John 6) and rescue from danger (Matthew 8:23-27) were interpreted as patronage. These "gifts" forged an implicit patron-client relationship. For this reason, the recipients of Jesus' benevolence praised their new patron and "news about him spread" (Matthew 4:24; Mark 1:28). Even when Jesus instructed people to keep silent, they could not refrain from broadcasting his benevolent deeds to others. Jesus' reputation as a benefactor increased with each miracle, causing more potential clients to seek his healing power.

Jesus' table fellowship with the marginalized also created patron-like social bonds. To the sinners and tax collectors, Jesus was a "friend," a term for patronage and local alliances (Luke 7:34; see also Luke 15:1-2; 19:7).[5] "In his earthly life Jesus was a benefactor especially of the oppressed, namely those outside the social and cultural mainstream."[6]

The Gospels recount the work of God's generous benefactions through Jesus. He provides the very benefits people sought from ancient benefactors: rescue and liberation from bondage (Matthew 8–9), forgiveness and amnesty (Matthew 9:2-6), life (Matthew 22:23-33), protection (Matthew 26:53), vindication (Matthew 27:50-54), praise and blessing (Matthew 5:1-12), food (Matthew 6:9-13), feasts (Matthew 14:13-21; 22:1-10), familial relations (Matthew 12:49-50), and peace (John 14:27).[7] As the Davidic king, Jesus mediates God's salvation to humanity. The benevolence of God comes

---

[4]There is admittedly no English verb for the Greek particle *euergetōn*, a linguistic issue discussed in the opening chapter. "Patronizing" has an entirely different meaning; the common translation of "doing good" misses the patronage dynamics; my choice of "benefacting" is not an actual word but serves the purpose here.

[5]Halvor Moxnes, "Patron-Client Relations and the New Community in Luke-Acts," in *The Social World of Luke-Acts: Models for Interpretation*, ed. Jerome H. Neyrey (Peabody, MA: Hendrickson Publishers, 1991), 258.

[6]Frederick W. Danker, *Benefactor: Epigraphic Study of a Greco-Roman and New Testament Semantic Field* (St. Louis, MO: Clayton Publishing House, 1982), 489.

[7]Adapted from Jerome H. Neyrey, "God, Benefactor and Patron: The Major Cultural Model for Interpreting the Deity in Greco-Roman Antiquity," *JSNT* 27, no. 4 (2005): 491.

through the ministry of Jesus (Luke 4:16-19). Anointed by the Spirit of God, Jesus bridges the gap between human needs and divine provisions. He brokers God's resources and grants access to God. Jesus' ministry was, in essence, benefaction.[8] In addition to mediating divine patronage to people, Jesus used the concept of patronage to communicate kingdom truths.

## PATRONAGE FOR KINGDOM TRUTHS

Imagine Jesus telling a parable like this one:

> Keith led a Christian ministry in Asia. He employed Donghai, a national believer, to manage local projects for the ministry organization. Keith began to hear rumors about Donghai misusing funds. So Keith summoned him, and asked, "What is this I hear about you? Tell me how you are spending the money, because you can no longer work here."
>
> Then Donghai said to himself, "What will I do, now that I am no longer employed by this international organization? I've worked there twenty-five years, so I have limited prospects for another job at my age. I am too ashamed to ask relatives for money, since I was always the person who helped them. I know what I will do, so that when I am dismissed in two weeks, people will welcome me into their homes!"
>
> Donghai secretly took 3,000 dollars from the organization's bank account and shared it with friends and family in the community. He told all of them that the money was from Keith to bless local families. Keith arrived at work the following day, completely unaware of what Donghai had done. Everyone had gathered at his office to thank Keith with words of praise for his generosity.
>
> When Keith realized what Donghai had done, he commended Donghai for acting so wisely and sensibly, "Usually unbelievers understand how to deal with these situations better than Christians. I tell you, it is good to build a relational network with unauthorized funds, so that you can depend on those relationships when the money runs out."

This story is a contemporary retelling of Jesus' parable about the Unjust Steward from Luke 16:1-8. Scholars all agree this parable is difficult to interpret. Why would the master commend the steward for being fraudulent? An understanding of patronage helps explain the point of Jesus' parable.

---

[8]David deSilva, *Honor, Patronage, Kinship & Purity* (Downers Grove, IL: IVP Academic, 2000), 133-34.

New Testament scholars David Landry and Ben May offer a viable interpretation in their article, "Honor Restored: New Light on the Parable of the Prudent Steward."[9] The steward's malfeasance made the master look foolish and weak in the community for being unable to control his household. So he fires the steward to save face. But the steward, facing a damaged reputation of his own, seeks to retain his own status in the community. "He uses his position as a broker to create patron-client links between himself and his master's tenants (16:4-7). By reducing their debts, they become indebted to him, and thus obliged to receive him as a guest in time of need."[10]

Moreover, this act of forgiving the debtors also restores the master's honor in the community. The debtors would praise the master's generosity far and wide, perhaps with a village feast in honor of the master. The master is obliged to recognize the debt reductions, because retracting his steward's offer would appear stingy and bring disgrace. Regardless, the master valued this newly gained honor more than the lost money. Therefore, the master esteems his steward for making him appear more honorable.

This patron-client interpretation also clarifies the parable's theological purpose. Why would Jesus promote malfeasance? Is this parable ethical instruction or some symbolic allegory?[11] A solution to this theological quandary is nearby. This parable of the "Admirable Client" (Luke 16:1-8) mirrors the preceding parable of the Prodigal Son (Luke 15:11-32). In both stories:

- An inferior person squanders property.
- Such malfeasance dishonors his superior.
- The inferior thus proposes a course of action to redeem himself from shame.
- Then the superior defies reason to welcome back the shamed inferior.

---

[9]David T. Landry and Ben May, "Honor Restored: New Light on the Parable of the Prudent Steward (Luke 16:1-8a)," *JBL* 119, no. 2 (2000): 287-309.

[10]Moxnes, "Patron-Client Relations," 253.

[11]The theological meaning of Luke 16:1-8 is illuminated by nearby passages. Scholars debate whether the following words about financial stewards (Luke 16:8-13) were Jesus' own explanation of the parable, or if Luke the author placed two separate teachings of Jesus side by side in his final redaction. The interpretation above favors the second option, though the first possibility would simply mirror Jesus' teaching in Luke 12:42-46.

The strong resemblance between these adjoining parables suggests we should interpret them together. In the parable of the Prudent Client, Jesus uses the model of patronage to teach the same kingdom truth as the Prodigal Son: those who honor God, regardless of past stigmas, are welcomed back into his household. That is, people who restore God's stained honor will themselves be honored. The two stories are about the redemption of shameful outcasts by a benevolent, honoring God.

In Luke 12:42-46 Jesus teaches his followers about being a "faithful" manager of God's resources. Jesus here refers to the ideology of patronage to teach about kingdom stewardship.

> And the Lord said, "Who then is the faithful and prudent manager whom his master will put in charge of his slaves, to give them their allowance of food at the proper time? Blessed is that slave whom his master will find at work when he arrives. Truly I tell you, he will put that one in charge of all his possessions. But if that slave says to himself, 'My master is delayed in coming,' and if he begins to beat the other slaves, men and women, and to eat and drink and get drunk, the master of that slave will come on a day when he does not expect him and at an hour that he does not know, and will cut him in pieces, and put him with the unfaithful."

Jesus' opening question introduces the idea of a faithful and prudent manager. "Faithful" (Greek: *pistos*) refers to a loyal and trustworthy person, and "prudent" is the same word (Greek: *phronimos*) used in parable of the Unjust Steward when the master commends his steward for acting "shrewdly" (Luke 16:8). The idea is a household manager who loyally defends the interests of his patron-master. Such a person is placed in a position of prominence over the master's other workers. Within networks of patronage, clients covet higher positions to receive preferential treatment from the patron. Jesus' description appeals to this hierarchical competitiveness among clients. The person busy working will be honored (Greek: *makarios*) with authority and clout. This loyal client is contrasted to the *un*faithful (Greek: *apistos*) worker who beats others and gets drunk, squandering his master's resources.

These two parables by Jesus assume a shared cultural knowledge about patronage. Jesus did not spell out the contours of patron-client relationships

but used patronage to teach theological truths. Like agriculture or construction, patronage was a plausible metaphor for explaining the nature of
God's kingdom.

## CRITIQUE OF MALEVOLENT PATRONS

On several occasions, Jesus denounces the wealthy and powerful for being
malevolent patrons. Jesus does not criticize the system of patronage but the
sinful abuse of the social system.

Jesus told parables about wealthy people who failed to share generously.
They consume extravagant resources but fail to help others.

> There was a rich man who was dressed in purple and fine linen and who feasted
> sumptuously every day. And at his gate lay a poor man named Lazarus, covered
> with sores, who longed to satisfy his hunger with what fell from the rich man's
> table; even the dogs would come and lick his sores. (Luke 16:19-21)

> The land of a rich man produced abundantly. And he thought to himself,
> "What should I do, for I have no place to store my crops?" Then he said, "I will
> do this: I will pull down my barns and build larger ones, and there I will store
> all my grain and my goods. And I will say to my soul, 'Soul, you have ample
> goods laid up for many years; relax, eat, drink, be merry.'" But God said to
> him, "You fool!" (Luke 12:16-20)

Both parables introduce a "rich man" who was unwilling to act as a benevolent patron within the community. At their death, they learn the fu-
tility of hoarding materials. These stories effectively critique "the rich" for
lacking the generosity expected of them.[12]

Jesus also rebukes the Jewish religious leaders for their warped view of
patronage. To the Pharisees who neglected justice, Jesus said, "Woe to you
Pharisees! For you love to have the seat of honor in the synagogues and to
be greeted with respect in the marketplaces" (Luke 11:43). They sought the
benefits of patronage (i.e., seats of honor and titles of respect) but avoided
the responsibilities of patronage (i.e., restoring and helping fellow Israelites). And when the Pharisees did share with others, they did so with a
calculated form of reciprocity. They only invited relatives or rich neighbors

---

[12]Moxnes, "Patron-Client Relations," 255.

who were capable of returning the favor (Luke 14:12). This behavior made them illegitimate benefactors in the eyes of God. Jesus accuses them of being "lovers of money," abusers of the oppressive structures of exploitation (Luke 16:14; cf. Luke 7:30). These words are "the total delegitimation of them as brokers" of God's favors.[13]

Though their financial patronage was corrupt, the Pharisees' main failure was as spiritual patrons over God's people. They blocked access to spiritual resources from the divine Patron. In the divine-human relationship, people have two main responsibilities towards God: obey and worship. Jews obeyed God by observing Torah and worshipped God at the temple. These were the primary channels for relating to God. The religious leaders who regulated Torah observance (Pharisees and scribes) and temple worship (Sadducees and priests), functioned as brokers in the patron-client relationship between God and Israelites. Unfortunately, both Pharisees and Sadducees blocked access to God and his salvation. The Pharisees used Torah to prevent Jesus' physical healings or marginalize law-breakers (Luke 5:21; 6:2, 7). The Sadducees charged steep admission fees to worship God at the temple (Matthew 21:12-17). For this reason, Jesus' critiques them as malevolent patrons. His criticism recalls Old Testament prophets who rebuked Israel's religious leaders as shepherds for fleecing the flock.

> Ah, you shepherds of Israel who have been feeding yourselves! Should not shepherds feed the sheep? You eat the fat, you clothe yourselves with the wool, you slaughter the fatlings; but you do not feed the sheep. You have not strengthened the weak, you have not healed the sick, you have not bound up the injured, you have not brought back the strayed, you have not sought the lost, but with force and harshness you have ruled them. So they were scattered, because there was no shepherd; and scattered, they became food for all the wild animals. (Ezekiel 34:2-5; cf. Jeremiah 23:1-2)

The language of shepherding evoked the expectations of patronage. Shepherds provide and protect; sheep listen and follow. The leaders were supposed to be benevolent patrons who shepherded Israel, but they

---

[13]Moxnes, "Patron-Client Relations," 256.

corrupted the system for personal gain. In the days of Ezekiel and Jeremiah, the shepherds (i.e., Israel's leaders) extorted and abandoned God's sheep. Jesus' denunciation of Jewish leaders echoed this blistering indictment of Israel's shepherds. His words against religious leaders were a prophetic critique of self-exalting, sheep-fleecing patrons.

## TRANSFORMING PATRONAGE

Jesus' scathing critique of bad patronage paves the way for a transformation of patron-client relationships. His critique of malevolent patrons implies that people should be benevolent patrons, not that patronage is itself bad. Jesus introduces a new model of patronage.

God's solution to bad patronage was to become Israel's shepherd himself and appoint a co-shepherd over Israel. God promised,

> I myself will search for my sheep, and will seek them out. As shepherds seek out their flocks when they are among their scattered sheep, so I will seek out my sheep. . . . I will set up over them one shepherd, my servant David, and he shall feed them: he shall feed them and be their shepherd. (Ezekiel 34:11-12, 23)

Jesus fulfills Ezekiel's promise of a benevolent patron who would provide and protect God's sheep. "I am the good shepherd. I know my own and my own know me" (John 10:14). Jesus, as the model patron, redefines three essential aspects of patronage: the patron, the gift, and the client.

*The patron.* The story of Jesus healing the centurion's servant in Luke 7 (see chapter two) is profoundly theological. Jesus' healing powers make a clear point. There is a new patron in town! Jesus' miracle subverts the traditional channels of benefaction in imperial Rome and places God atop the social hierarchy. The centurion made his living by honoring Caesar in Rome to ensure access to favors. But now he faces a problem that Caesar could not solve, a sick servant. To access health care, the centurion turns to another patron who could heal. Jesus' healing subverts Rome's imperial narrative—"Rome brings peace, prosperity, and protection to humanity"— and introduces a new King worthy of following. The demonstration of Jesus' healing power calls for a shift in allegiances, away from the imperial patronal system that flowed down from Caesar and to the newly available patronage system that began with the ultimate patron—God the Father, known through his Son Jesus.[14]

The Gospels present God as the ideal and supreme benefactor who uses his power to benefit the lowly and marginalized. Mary's song praised God for his favors towards her. In blessing Mary with a special child, God demonstrates his trustworthiness as Israel's patron. And so she says:

> My soul magnifies the Lord, and my spirit rejoices in God my Savior,
> for he has looked with favor on the lowliness of his servant. . . .
> He has brought down the powerful from their thrones, and lifted up
>     the lowly;
> he has filled the hungry with good things, and sent the rich away empty.
> He has helped his servant Israel, in remembrance of his mercy,
> according to the promise he made to our ancestors, to Abraham and to his
>     descendants forever. (Luke 1:46-48; 52-55)

The patronage of God creates new relational expectations. Jesus said, "No slave can serve two masters; for a slave will either hate the one and love the other, or be devoted to the one and despise the other. You cannot serve God and wealth" (Luke 16:13). The Old Testament language of patronage fills this verse: patronage relationships were between *masters* and *slaves*; the language of love, devotion, and service referred to clients' allegiance; and to hate or despise meant relational disloyalty (see chapter four). The fact that God is the highest patron redefines our relationships and redirects our allegiance. Earthly patrons are in fact clients under God's provision and, at most, brokers who mediate God's graces to other people. (Later chapters examine how the early church redefines human patronage in such a way for Christians.)

***The gift.*** Jesus also redefines the very meaning of benefaction. "The greatness traditionally associated with the role of the patron is now intimately linked with the act of serving."[15] God's kingdom changes the nature and motivation of benevolence. Extending patronage towards other people is not a means to acquiring honor or authority, but an expression of thankfulness towards God.

---

[14]Jayson Georges and Mark D. Baker, *Ministering in Honor-Shame Cultures: Biblical Foundations and Practical Essentials* (Downers Grove, IL: IVP Academic, 2016), 153.
[15]Moxnes, "Patron-Client Relations," 260.

Jesus asked the disciples, "For who is greater, the one who is at the table or the one who serves? Is it not the one at the table?" (Luke 22:27). This questioning refers to the custom of the honored guests reclining at the table while the socially inferior serve them. Jesus overturns that imagery with an unexpected answer, "But I am among you as one who serves." Jesus does not position himself in the honored seat but behind the water jar (cf. Luke 12:37). Jesus' patronage-leadership is founded on service and sharing, not extracting.

Jesus' only explicit mention of benefaction (or patronage) occurs in Luke 22:25-26, a verse commonly misread as a blanket critique of benefaction. The NRSV reads, "The kings of the Gentiles lord it over them; and those in authority over them are called benefactors. But not so with you; rather the greatest among you must become like the youngest, and the leader like one who serves." Commentators assume this verse "speaks of *tyrannical* rulers who only *masquerade* as benefactors."[16] However, this reading was probably not Jesus' original intention.

The disciples' question, "Who is the greatest?" (see Luke 22:24) asks who will have the greatest honor and social precedence. In his answer, Jesus provides a new pathway to honor and new ideal for benefactors—serving others. Jesus' first comment addresses their concern by stating a fact, "The Gentiles' kings rule, and those with authority are called 'benefactors,' but not so with you" (Luke 22:25, author's own translation). Jesus' final comment "but not so with you" does not negate all titles, nor preclude the possibility of them becoming a benefactor.[17] Rather than prescribing what the disciples *should* not be, Jesus merely *describes* that the disciples are not (yet) honorable benefactors, great in the eyes of others. And more importantly, the pathway to achieve the aspirational title of "the greatest" is using power to benefit and serve others. Jesus says the honorable benefactors and great leaders are to become like the youngest, the one who serves (Luke 22:26-27). Then in the

---

[16]David John Lull, "The Servant-Benefactor as a Model of Greatness (Luke 22:24-30)," *NovT* 28:4 (October 1986): 290. Italics original.

[17]Jesus is stating the fact that his disciples are not called "benefactors." The phrase is not prescriptive, as some translations incorrectly suggest by adding verbs such as "to be" (NIV) or "shall" (KJV), despite the lack of any such verb in Greek. While most translations follow the pattern of NIV or KJV by adding some sort of prescriptive verb, the ESV and NET use the language of "not so with you."

age to come, Jesus will reward his loyal servants who stand by him (Luke 22:28). He will transfer his sovereign rule to them (Luke 22:29) and recognize their greatness (Luke 22:30). Instead of assuming authority and giving to accrue honor in this age, Jesus' followers are called to serve others, and by giving *this* particular benefit they will receive divine honors in the age to come.

Rather than being an anti-hierarchical denunciation of benefaction, this verse reveals the path to true benefaction and greatness in God's kingdom. In sum, Jesus' teaching about a servant-benefactor continues the Old Testament theme of biblical patronage as being life giving. The honorable status of patronage comes by giving to (not, taking from) clients who need help. True patronage looks to serve, not to be served.

*The client.* The recipients of Jesus' benevolence were the people most in need of help. He ate with tax collectors and sinners, and he healed the sick and demonized. He gave favors to those incapable of reciprocating. In word and deed, Jesus redefined the clients of true patronage. The recipients of his benefaction were not well-capitalized people who could return favors.

Jesus' uncalculated generosity introduces another characteristic (along with God-centered and life-giving) of biblical patronage: unworthy grace. This means gifts are granted to unqualified, undeserving clients; grace is given without regard to one's worth. This principle is a contrast to the common practice of patrons who give in a self-interested manner to acquire status and honor. Jesus not only made a practice of extending such grace to the unworthy, he taught his disciples to do likewise.

> If you do good to those who do good to you, what credit is that to you? For even sinners do the same. If you lend to those from whom you hope to receive, what credit is that to you? Even sinners lend to sinners, to receive as much again. But love your enemies, do good, and lend, expecting nothing in return. (Luke 6:33-35)

> When you give a luncheon or a dinner, do not invite your friends or your brothers or your relatives or rich neighbors, in case they may invite you in return, and you would be repaid. But when you give a banquet, invite the poor, the crippled, the lame, and the blind. (Luke 14:12-13)

Giving without expecting a return is inconceivable in traditional patronage, for reciprocity was socially mandatory. Jesus knew these expectations of reciprocity were hardwired into the disciples' worldview. So he does not spurn all notions of repayment, but redefines the return payment. Jesus promises spiritual repayment to those who give such unworthy grace.

> You will be blessed, because they cannot repay you, for you will be repaid at the resurrection of the righteous. (Luke 14:14)
> Your reward will be great, and you will be children of the Most High. (Luke 6:35)

In the framework of biblical patronage, eschatological greatness from God *is* the repayment we shall receive for generosity. God rewards patrons in eternity. This promise removes any expectation of repayment from clients. Because God will reciprocate our giving, we are to be merciful just like God, even to ungrateful people (Luke 6:35-36).

## CONCLUSION

Jesus redefines the cores elements of patronage. He does not dismantle patronage in favor of a twenty-first-century democracy marked by social equality and individual rights. Such Enlightenment values would have been inexpressible in the first-century world. Rather, Jesus preserves the general institution of patronage, but transforms it to be *God-centered*, *life-giving*, and *grace-unworthy*.

# 6

# PAUL AND THE CHURCH

PATRONAGE WAS AN INESCAPABLE REALITY FOR PAUL as he proclaimed the gospel and formed communities in the first-century Roman world. The costs of his traveling, housing, and letter writing required significant financial generosity. And a significant part of his apostolic ministry was collecting financial gifts from the Gentile churches for the poorer Jerusalem church. So issues of patronage—e.g., gifts, favors, reciprocity, and social debt—would have been unavoidable issues in his ministry.[1]

While Paul challenged certain aspects of patronage, he always worked *within* the cultural system and navigated the contours of patronage. "Paul wasn't opposed to the patronage system; he probably couldn't image a world without it."[2] Paul leveraged patronage in his ministry relationships and discipled Gentile converts into a biblical view of both patronage and clientage. This chapter explores four areas of his ministry affected by patronage: raising missionary support, the Philippians' gift, the Jerusalem collection, and Christian benefactors.

## MISSIONARY SUPPORT

Did Paul reject or accept "missionary support" from other people? The answer is both yes and no. In some instances Paul boasted in not receiving money, yet on other occasions he *requested* financial help for his ministry. Paul's nuanced view of patronage clarifies his seemingly inconsistent view on missionary support. On several occasions Paul refused financial

---

[1]David E. Briones, *Paul's Financial Policy: A Socio-Theological Approach* (London: Bloomsbury T&T Clark, 2015), 21.
[2]E. Randolph Richards and Brandon J. O'Brien, *Misreading Scripture with Western Eyes: Removing Cultural Blinders to Better Understand the Bible* (Downers Grove, IL: IVP Books, 2012), 165.

patronage and supported himself as a leatherworker/tent-maker (cf. Acts 18:1-3). Here are two examples.

- You remember our labor and toil, brothers and sisters; we worked night and day, so that we might not burden any of you while we proclaimed to you the gospel of God. (1 Thessalonians 2:9; cf. 2 Thessalonians 3:8)

- And when I was with you and was in need, I did not burden anyone, for my needs were supplied by the friends who came from Macedonia. So I refrained and will continue to refrain from burdening you in any way. (2 Corinthians 11:9; cf. 1 Corinthians 9:12)

This was countercultural in several ways. Paul could have added legitimacy to his ministry by accepting financial help. Association with a prominent patron would have enhanced Paul's reputation as an itinerant speaker. Nevertheless, Paul chose to work with his hands as a leatherworker. Such manual labor was considered shameful, especially for public teachers such as Paul. Leatherworking was itself a stigma, plus the meager income led to an impoverished, disgraceful lifestyle. Paul says, "To the present hour we are hungry and thirsty, we are poorly clothed and beaten and homeless, and we grow weary from the work of our own hands. . . . We have become like the rubbish of the world, the dregs of all things, to this very day" (1 Corinthians 4:11, 13, cf. 2 Corinthians 11:27). Paul's rejection of financial patronage caused him tremendous shame. So, why did he choose this option? Paul's convictions about patronage best explain why he occasionally refused missionary support.

Paul deduced that accepting benefaction would hinder his ministry.[3] Receiving the gift would have obliged Paul as a dependent client to a wealthy patron, and he did not want to become a trophy for an

---

[3]We cannot know the motivation behind Paul's choice to work as a leatherworker. Verlyn Verbrugge and Keith R. Krell, *Paul and Money: A Biblical and Theological Analysis of the Apostle's Teachings and Practices* (Grand Rapids: Zondervan, 2015), 59-60, note how the stated reason in his letters to the Thessalonians and Corinthians (i.e., to not burden them and be an example) could not have been Paul's original reason. Rather, Paul mentions the example of his manual labor as an ad hoc argument to motivate the Christians there, but chose to support himself before those incidents. However, they stretch the bounds of responsible exegesis with their psychological speculation that Paul opted to suffer because of a "guilt-complex" for persecuting Christians. The dynamics of patronage mentioned in this chapter are a factor (though not *the* reason) in Paul's rationale for not accepting finances.

honor-seeking patron. He would not allow his ministry to be hijacked for the glory of an earthly patron.

While Paul avoided controlling patrons, he also avoided dependent clients in Corinth. Paul refused money from toadyish students in new cities.[4] This act disassociated Paul from other itinerant philosophers who exploited followers to enhance their own honor and status. Paul did not want his client-students to lionize him. Rather, he was a "slave of God" who mediated divine favors free of charge. The young churches were not to repay Paul as a revered teacher but redirect their thanks and loyalty to God as the original source of all favors.

Paul rebuffed money from both wealthy patrons and groveling students in Corinth. This avoided the social pitfalls of being either an obligated client of would-be benefactors or the glory-receiving patron of indebted disciples. Paul corrects the Corinthians' cultural practice of using connections to accrue honor and status. The source of the Corinthians' honor was not their relationship with Paul (as either his patron or his client) but their connection with God. Paul refused their patronage in order to disciple the immature, culturally influenced Corinthians. Their warped view of patronage distorted the gospel of God's benevolence; God graced sinners with salvation *regardless* of their status, not *because* of their status. Paul overturns conventional thinking by boasting in shame (2 Corinthians 11:30) and inviting the Corinthians to become co-laborers in the ministry which recognized God as the ultimate giver.[5]

However, Paul did not *always* reject financial patronage. His words to the Corinthians reflect a temporary, not permanent, financial policy. Their spiritual immaturity prevented Paul from leveraging the patron-client paradigm for redemptive purposes, but that was not always the case. Paul often accepted—and even requested—monetary gifts. In the context of

---

[4]For more support on Paul's refusal to play the patronizing role of itinerate teachers, see Briones, *Paul's Financial Policy*, 163-67. Briones pits his student-pupil framework (wherein the money was payment from inferior students) against the traditional patronal interpretation of Paul (wherein the money was benefaction from superior patrons). But the social inequality of ancient Rome suggests the Corinthian church included both wealthy patrons and opportunistic students. The pursuit of honor (*philotimia*) compelled both groups in their respective ways, leaving Paul to fend off warped patronage from both sides.

[5]Briones, *Paul's Financial Policy*, 190.

Greco-Roman patronage, these funds created a social debt of obligation.[6] Paul's practice of requesting financial help "is a recognition that Paul lived in the Greco-Roman world with its encouragement of reciprocity for favors received, and at times he could work comfortably within that system without compromising his loyalty to the principles of the gospel."[7] Here are five instances of Paul receiving financial help.

- Philemon. Paul requested housing assistance from Philemon: "One thing more [while I'm making requests]—prepare a guest room for me" (Philemon 22).

- Lydia. After Lydia was baptized, Paul and his team accept room and board from her (Acts 16:15).

- Phoebe. Paul says Phoebe was "a benefactor of many and of myself as well" (Romans 16:2).

- "Sending" churches. Paul asks the church in Rome to send him on his way to Spain (Romans 15:24). The verb *propempō* has a specific meaning of "help on one's journey," like the contemporary phrase "missionary support." He expected Christians (cf. 1 Corinthians 16:6; 2 Corinthians 1:16; Titus 3:13) to participate in his mission by providing necessary support when he moved to new places.

- Sponsors for letters. The cost of communicating in antiquity was staggering. For example, producing a letter the length of Romans cost over $2,000 in present-day dollars.[8] Greco-Roman patrons financed the living and writing expenses of authors, and this sponsorship enhanced their status. The significant costs of writing letters "could only have come from a patron of some sort—and that would mean that Paul likely had to ask for money from someone to fund such a project."[9]

Paul rejected financial help from some churches but exhorted other churches to support gospel workers and requested personal support. Paul's transformed view of patronage explains this apparent contradiction. Paul refused money

---

[6]This list and the subsequent conclusions summarize Verbrugge and Krell, *Paul and Money*, 81-103.
[7]Verbrugge and Krell, *Paul and Money*, 91.
[8]E. Randolph Richards, *Paul and First-Century Letter Writing: Secretaries, Composition, and Collection* (Downers Grove, IL: IVP Academic, 2004), 165-69.
[9]Verbrugge and Krell, *Paul and Money*, 102.

from unbelievers in new locations and from immature Christians because their worldly conceptions of patronage would spoil their relationship with Paul and the very nature of God's grace. But once a church was established, he welcomed their financial participation in the spread of the gospel.

Paul cultivated patronage relationships with affluent Christians, but those relationships did not mirror cultural norms for patron-client relationships. Paul viewed his reciprocal relationships with fellow Christians as ones of "friendship."[10] This type of friendship in ancient cultures retained clear expectations of reciprocity and mutual benefit; both sides protected each other's interests as allies.[11] Paul's requests for financial assistance formed a reciprocal friendship with spiritual equals. Their relationship was based on their spiritual identity as brothers and sisters in Christ, not their sociocultural status. Their mutual calling in the gospel formed the basis of their mutual obligation. Oppressive inequality and self-serving manipulation characterized worldly patronage, but Paul rejected those patterns in his missional relationships with early churches. Healthy patron-client relationships were possible because Paul discipled early Christians into a transformed view of patronage, as seen in 2 Corinthians 8–9 and Philippians 4.

## THE JERUSALEM COLLECTION (2 CORINTHIANS 8–9)

Paul expended significant time and energy collecting money from the Gentile churches for the impoverished church in Jerusalem. The importance and international scope of the project suggests a large amount of funds. Patronage influenced the Jerusalem collection in several ways, as the money would have evoked the standard expectations of reciprocity.

Paul writes 2 Corinthians to prepare the church for his upcoming visit. The letter shows Paul's concern for their social divisions, theological immaturity, and financial unpreparedness. Their contributions for the Jerusalem collection are behind target and must be brought up to speed before his arrival. Paul has a contentious relationship with the Corinthians but desires their contribution to the Jerusalem collection. Paul walks this

---

[10]This is a simple description of Roman "friendship." For more, see Verbrugge and Krell, *Paul and Money*, 90-91.

[11]Verbrugge and Krell, *Paul and Money*, 85-86.

relational tightrope in 2 Corinthians 8–9, where he uses their assumptions about patronage to motivate giving—but not without transforming their misconceptions about patronage.

To motivate the Corinthians' giving, Paul employs the social logic of patronage in three different ways. First, Paul uses the Greek word *charis* eleven times in his discussion on financial giving (2 Corinthians 8:1, 2, 4, 6, 7, 9, 16, 19; 9:8, 14, 15). In Paul's day *charis* referred to the gifts that patrons and clients exchanged, a tangible response of gratitude to benevolence (see chapter nine). Paul uses *charis* as a euphemism for their contribution. This word choice purposefully evoked the system of patronage and grants a specific social meaning to their financial benevolence. The standard English translation of *charis* as "grace" mutes the ancient dynamics of patronage. Some translations better capture the connotations of patronage of the word *charis:* "generous undertaking" (NRSV), "act of grace" (NIV), or "relief offering" (MSG).

Second, Paul tells the Corinthians that their honor is in jeopardy. Paul has been boasting about the Corinthians' generosity to other churches. That boasting created a certain reputation the Corinthians would have been motivated to uphold.

> I am sending the brothers in order that our boasting about you may not prove
> to have been empty in this case, so that you may be ready, as I said you would
> be; otherwise, if some Macedonians come with me and find that you are not
> ready, we would be humiliated—to say nothing of you—in this undertaking.
> (2 Corinthians 9:3-4)

If the Corinthians do not collect the money, they will face shame. The appeal to honor and shame—the key motives of patronage—is blatant. Paul's "shameless request" (to use our modern language) for money is perfectly logical and honorable within the framework of patronage.

Third, 2 Corinthians 9:8 uses common language about benefaction to exhort the church. The verse could read: "God is powerful enough to provide you with abundant benevolence, so that you never have any need and can abundantly gift those resources to others."[12]

---

[12]Much like *charis*, the phrase "good work" was a reference to patronage. This is explained below in the section "Early Christians as Public Benefactors."

In sum, the repetition of *charis*, the threat of shame (2 Corinthians 9:4), and the language of benefaction (2 Corinthians 9:8) all evoke the framework of patronage to define the Corinthians' role in the Jerusalem collection. Paul uses patronage to interpret the meaning of their financial gift. But in the process, he also challenges the Corinthians' assumptions about patronage.

Paul introduces a God-centered view of patronage wherein reciprocal exchanges are part of a larger relational eco-system. According to social conventions, the Corinthians were entitled to praise and thanks for the gift. Paul corrects these assumptions with two theological facts: the gift originated *from* God (2 Corinthians 9:8-10), so consequently the praise belongs *to* God (2 Corinthians 9:11-15). The passage of 2 Corinthians 9:8-10 four times reiterates the point that the gift is from God, not from the Corinthians.

> And *God is able* to provide you with every blessing in abundance, so that by always having enough of everything, you may share abundantly in every good work. As it is written,
>
> "*He* scatters abroad, *he* gives to the poor;
> *his* benevolence endures forever."
>
> *He* who supplies seed to the sower and bread for food will supply and multiply your seed for sowing and increase the harvest of your benevolence.[13]
> (2 Corinthians 9:8-10, emphasis added)

And because God initiates the gift, he receives the praise. The Corinthians' generosity produces thanks to God, not an increase of their own status. Paul and the Jerusalem recipients will worship God for the Corinthians' "indescribable gift." This thanksgiving to God is prominent in each verse of 2 Corinthians 9:11-15 (italics added):

> You will be enriched in every way for your great generosity, which will produce *thanksgiving to God* through us; for the rendering of this ministry not only supplies the needs of the saints but also overflows with *many thanksgivings to God*. Through the testing of this ministry *you glorify God* by your obedience to the confession of the gospel of Christ and by the generosity of your sharing with them and with all others, while they long for you and pray for you

---

[13]NRSV footnotes in 2 Cor 9:9, 10 indicate that *dikaiosynē* can be translated as "benevolence" as well as "righteousness." This citation inserts that translation option.

because of the surpassing grace of God that he has given you. *Thanks be to God*
for his indescribable gift!

Paul transforms the meaning of the Corinthians' gift by situating it within
a larger framework. Paul introduces God as a third party in the exchange
(see figure 6.1). This reframes the Corinthians' perspective on patronage
and the meaning of their gift to the Jerusalem offering.[14]

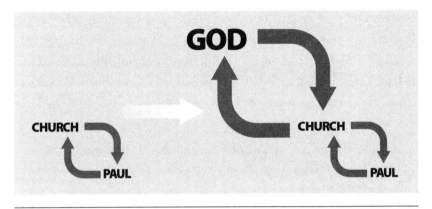

**Figure 6.1.** Paul's transformed patronage

### THE PHILIPPIANS' GIFT (PHILIPPIANS 4)

Paul addresses issues of money and honor in his relationship with believers
in Philippi. The letter of Philippians is a "missionary support letter." Paul
acknowledges the funds that the church sent through Epaphroditus, but
Paul's response is rather unconventional. He does not explicitly thank the
Philippians but offers a sort of "thankless thank-you."[15]

Paul rejoices in the Philippians "concern" for him (Philippians 4:10-11)
but explains that their gift was not essential for him (Philippians 4:12-13).
The Philippians' gift is helpful, says Paul, but it does not affect his

---

[14]The gospel transforms human patronage in other significant ways. Relationships now have a different
goal—participating in the forward advance of God's gracious love. The act of giving enjoins us in Christ's
gifting to others. Furthermore, the good acquired through patronage is no longer social advancement
and resources but co-sharing in Jesus' life and in the advance of the gospel. Giving funds is also for the
benefit of the Corinthians; by stewarding the funds in such a manner as to generate praise, the Corinthians, albeit indirectly, fulfill their own obligations of bringing honor to their divine patronage.

[15]Cf. David Briones, "Paul's Intentional 'Thankless Thanks' in Philippians 4.10-20," *JSNT* 34, no. 1
(Sept 2011): 47-69.

circumstances since he has learned to be content regardless of circumstances. While God certainly worked through the Philippians to meet Paul's need, God remains Paul's ultimate provider. Much like 2 Corinthians 8–9, Philippians 4 situates the exchange in the broader system of divine patronage— God is the central figure *from* whom and *to* him all things flows.

Paul then mentions how their repeated kindness was unparalleled (Philippians 4:14-16), but quickly pivots to reframe their conceptions of patronage (Philippians 4:17-20). Philippians 4:17-20 offers a nuanced reflection on Christian patronage. These verses contrast human-centered patronage with God-centered patronage in four key areas: the repayment, the gift, the source, and the recipient of praise (see table 6.1).

| ASPECT OF PATRONAGE | HUMAN-CENTERED PATRONAGE | GOD-CENTERED PATRONAGE |
| --- | --- | --- |
| Repayment (4:17) | Client indebted to repay the patron | God spiritually repays the patron |
| Gift (4:18) | Given from patron to client | Offered as a sacrifice to God |
| Source (4:19) | The patron shares their wealth | God provides all riches |
| Recipient of Praise (4:20) | The patron who gave money | God as the Creator |

**Table 6.1.** Paul's God-centered patronage in Philippians

Paul first says, "Not that I seek the gift, but I seek the profit that accumulates to your account" (Philippians 4:17). Patrons in the ancient world expected repayment, but Paul eliminates any notion of debt. The Philippians' gift did not obligate Paul since they were already compensated. God himself (not Paul) repays the gift by adding credit to their spiritual account (cf. Luke 6:35; 14:14).

Paul also explains the spiritual meaning of their money. "I have received from Epaphroditus the gifts you sent, a fragrant offering, a sacrifice acceptable and pleasing to God" (Philippians 4:18). Their gift was not merely a financial contribution to Paul but an act of worship to God. In the Old Testament temple, offerings were a gift to God. The cultic metaphor defines the Philippians' gift as worship. This echoes the wisdom of Proverbs 19:17, "Whoever is kind to the poor lends to the LORD, and will be repaid in full."

Then Philippians 4:19 redefines the actual source of the gift. "And my God will fully satisfy every need of yours according to his riches in glory in

Christ Jesus" (Philippians 4:19). The money Paul received was not from the Philippians. The church in Philippi is not a patron to Paul but a broker who stewards God's riches. Miroslav Volf says that Paul "doesn't thank [the Philippians] directly because he believes that he hasn't received gifts *from* them but *through* them. The giver is God. They are his channels."[16]

Finally, Paul explains the end purpose of the exchange. "To our God and Father be glory forever and ever. Amen" (Philippians 4:20). The customs of patronage would have tempted the Philippians to expect certain honors from Paul. But he redirects the praise toward God. God alone receives the praise and glory for the gift. God is the beginning and end of all gifts.

In Philippians 4, Paul explains how the gospel redefines patronage. This recalculation has profound implications for the community in Philippi. "Grace cascades from God the patron, flows in, through and among participants 'in Christ,' and eventually returns back as *eucharistia* [thanks/praise] to God, the supreme giver."[17]

### EARLY CHRISTIANS AS PUBLIC BENEFACTORS

Some early Christians came from higher socioeconomic classes. Before conversion they were patrons who used their affluence for public benefaction. Paul encourages these believers to continue as public benefactors.

In Romans 13:3, Paul offers a general instruction about public benefaction: "Then do what is good, and you will receive its approval." The Greek phrase "do good" in this verse does not refer to general morality, as Westerners might assume. Bruce Winter's article "The Public Honoring of Christian Benefactors: Romans 13:3-4 and 1 Peter 2:14-15" shows this verse echoes the precise language of ancient benefaction. Archeologists have uncovered many stone inscriptions that publicly honor patrons for their benefactions.[18] When clients erected these inscriptions,

---

[16]Miroslav Volf, *Free of Charge: Giving and Forgiving in a Culture Stripped of Grace* (Grand Rapids: Zondervan, 2006), 112-13.

[17]Briones, "Paul's Intentional 'Thankless Thanks,'" 63-4. See also, David deSilva, *Honor, Patronage, Kinship & Purity: Unlocking New Testament Culture* (Downers Grove, IL: IVP Academic), 152-54.

[18]For a translated collection of 51 ancient inscriptions for benefaction, see Frederick W. Danker, *Benefactor: Epigraphic Study of a Greco-Roman and New Testament Semantic Field* (St. Louis, MO: Clayton Publishing House, 1982).

they used specific terms to describe the reciprocal exchange. For example, "good" (*agathon*) was a common term for public benefaction, and "praise/approval" (*epainon*) was the reward promised to such benefactors. Paul's deliberate wording in Romans 13:4 "reflected a long-established social custom of appropriate recognition of public benefactors."[19] By using the language found on public instructions, Paul not only encourages wealthy Christians to act as benefactors but also promises them public praise as an incentive.[20] In Romans 13 and 1 Peter 2, the apostles endorsed "ethical conduct expressed in high-profile good works." The rationale behind the apostles' endorsement of sociopolitical benefaction was not acceptance for acculturation purposes, but to bring good to their fellow citizens by meeting needs.[21]

Beyond the general instruction of Romans 13:3-4, Paul affirms a specific benefactor in the Christian community. He introduces Phoebe to the church in Rome with these words:

> I commend to you our sister Phoebe, a deacon of the church at Cenchreae, so that you may welcome her in the Lord as is fitting for the saints, and help her in whatever she may require from you, for she has been a benefactor of many and of myself as well. (Romans 16:1-2)

Phoebe was Paul's personal messenger who delivered Paul's letter to Rome. Since she was unknown to the Romans, Paul commends her as a respectable person whom they should welcome.[22] Paul calls Phoebe a "benefactor [*prostatis*] of many and of myself" (Romans 16:2). The Greek word *prostatis* "was also used to translate the Latin word *patronus*, which means "patron or benefactor," so that *prostatis* can also mean 'patroness.'"[23] Bibles that translate *prostatis* as "helper/helpful" (e.g., NASB, NKJV, NLT) suggest

---

[19]Bruce W. Winter, "The Public Honouring of Christian Benefactors: Romans 13:3-4 and 1 Peter 2:14-15," *JSNT*, no. 34 (1988): 90.
[20]Paul's promise of social status to Christian benefactors does, on the surface, appear to contradict Jesus' words about the praise being in the afterlife and Paul's own strategy of diverting praise from the human giver to God. Perhaps Paul assumed the Christian benefactor would responsibly steward earthly honor to bring about more social flourishing.
[21]Winter, "The Public Honouring," 95-96.
[22]Verbrugge and Krell, *Paul and Money*, 95.
[23]Verbrugge and Krell, *Paul and Money*, 95.

that Phoebe served as Paul's secretarial assistant. However, her help was actually social clout and financial largess.[24]

Phoebe provided vital help to many people, including the apostle Paul himself. Her patronage likely included sponsoring the writing of Paul's letter; serving as a legal/political representative for the Christian community; and opening her home for worship gatherings and visiting Christians. For her patronage, Paul introduces her as his *prostatis*, a term of honor. Paul's endorsement of Phoebe's role in the ministry indicates he supported public benefaction by affluent Christians.

## CONCLUSION

Issues like missionary support, the Jerusalem collection, and discipling churches required Paul to navigate patronage. In his ministry relationships, Paul leveraged patronal dynamics to reflect kingdom truths and promoted patronage in the early Christian community. Along with Yahweh in the Old Testament and Jesus in the Gospels, Paul's life and letters illustrates the pervasiveness of patronage in biblical theology. Throughout the Bible, patronage is not merely a social reality that shapes relationships but also a theological reality that explains the very essence of the gospel, as we examine in the next section.

---

[24]English translations are now adopting the language of "benefactor" (NIV, NRSV) and "patron/ess" (ESV, OJB).

PART THREE

# THEOLOGICAL CONCEPTS

# 7

# GOD AS PATRON

IN THE BIBLE, humans have a patron-client relationship with God. Patronage was the natural paradigm for biblical writers to use when explaining the gospel. In *Misreading Scripture with Western Eyes*, Richards and O'Brien explain,

> Because it was impossible to escape the patronage system, Paul worked within it, even in his explanation of the Christian message of salvation. . . . When Paul sought to explain the Christian's new relationship with God, then, one of the ways he did so was in terms of the ancient system of patronage—something everyone understood.[1]

Frederick Danker states that the apostles used the benefactor model "to bridge Jewish and Greco-Roman culture and to communicate the significance of Jesus Christ."[2] In light of this reality, the following three chapters use patronage to examine key aspects of Christian theology—God, sin, and salvation. The Bible presents God as a patron, sin as ungrateful clientage, and salvation as divine patronage.

A theology framed in terms of patronage does not deny or replace historic Christian theology. The realities of God, sin, and salvation require multiple metaphors to capture their full complexity. For example, God is a "father," "shepherd," "rock," and more. Patronage is another conceptual metaphor biblical authors used to explain the glorious truths of the spiritual world. The notion that God is a patron compliments and enhances Christian theology by emphasizing biblical concepts often overlooked in Western theology but readily familiar to people in collectivistic cultures.

---

[1]E. Randolph Richards and Brandon J. O'Brien, *Misreading Scripture with Western Eyes: Removing Cultural Blinders to Better Understand the Bible* (Downers Grove, IL: IVP Books, 2012), 166.

[2]Frederick W. Danker, *Benefactor: Epigraphic Study of a Greco-Roman and New Testament Semantic Field* (St. Louis, MO: Clayton Publishing House, 1982), 28.

## DIVINE PATRONAGE

Biblical writers assumed God is *the* true Patron. Yahweh was Israel's patron
in the Old Covenant (chapter four). Both Jesus and Paul appropriate social
patronage in their ministry, but modify it to account for God as the ultimate source of patronage for the human family (chapters five and six).

The patron-client relationship provided a consistent model for New Testament authors to describe God. According to Greek linguist Frederick
Danker, "The profile of the Greco-Roman benefactor dominates in the
presentations of God that are set forth in the New Testament."[3] God and
Jesus were "benefactors par excellence, whose generosity, even to the point
of suffering, fulfilled the Greco-Roman ideal and simultaneously challenged the system."[4] Early Christians viewed God as *the* Patron, not just
*a* patron. This chapter will clarify the identity of God as a patron in a more
systematic fashion.

## NEW TESTAMENT LANGUAGE OF PATRONAGE

Sociolinguistic research reveals how the New Testament depicts God as a
patron. Jerome Neyrey states that benefactor/patron was "the major cultural model for interpreting the deity in Greco-Roman antiquity."[5] People
in the first-century Mediterranean world "saw their gods as patrons and
benefactors and their own conduct as clients."[6] The ancients used multiple
technical titles to express benefaction. "All of these names directly communicate that God shows various types of favor, blessing, benefaction and
patronage to mortals."[7] Interestingly, the New Testament applies those *same*
titles to God the Father and Jesus. Here is a summary list of five keys titles
for benefactors in ancient Greek, along with a brief explanation of each
term and New Testament examples.

---

[3]Danker, *Benefactor*, 493.
[4]This summary of Danker, *Benefactor* is from Jonathan Marshall, *Jesus, Patrons, and Benefactors: Roman Palestine and the Gospel of Luke* (Tübingen: Mohr Siebeck, 2009), 2.
[5]Jerome H. Neyrey, "God, Benefactor and Patron: The Major Cultural Model for Interpreting the Deity in Greco-Roman Antiquity," *JSNT* 27, no. 4 (June 2005): 465-92; *Render to God: New Testament Understandings of the Divine* (Minneapolis: Fortress, 2004).
[6]Zeba A. Crook, *Reconceptualising Conversion: Patronage, Loyalty, and Conversion in the Religions of the Ancient Mediterranean* (New York: De Gruyter, 2004), 254.
[7]Neyrey, "God, Benefactor and Patron," 490. The bullet points summarize pages 471-74.

1. King (*basileus*). Greeks spoke about gods as "kings" when referring to the positive results of their rule. The Gospels speak about God's "kingdom" and the attending benefits; God is King (1 Timothy 1:17; Revelation 15:3; 19:16).

2. Father (*patēr*). For both Greeks and Hebrews, this familial term applied to political benefactors. The Roman word for patron (*patronus*) derives from this word. "Father" is a prominent New Testament title for God (Matthew 6:9-12; Ephesians 1:3; 3:14-16; Galatians 4:6).

3. Savior (*sotēr*). A savior would rescue, protect, bless, and benefit others. The term referred to a powerful person praised for delivering a community from invasion or peril. "Savior" is a common title for Jesus in the New Testament (Luke 1:47; 1 Timothy 1:1; 2:3; 3:4, 6; 4:10; Jude 25).

4. Benefactor (*euergetēs*). The term "benefactor," often coupled with "savior," describes someone who provides material benefit to those in need. The *euerg-* word family refers to God fourteen times in the Septuagint.[8]

5. Master/Sovereign (*despotēs*). The term for a slave's master was used to petition a person with power. Christians used the term to denote divine power and benevolence. God is Master (Luke 2:29; Acts 4:24).

The New Testament also applies the *characteristics* of benefactors to God. Ancient writers attributed a common set of moral attributes to patrons. They used certain terms, phrases, and formulations for people and gods whose contributions benefited humanity.[9] In the book *Benefactor: An Epigraphic Study of a Graeco-Roman and New Testament Field*, Frederick Danker notes how the New Testament adopts the very language of Greco-Roman benefaction to describe the character and actions of God. Examples include these: virtue, goodness, good, do good, offer oneself, save, kindness, give freely, righteousness, and faith/faithfulness.

Greco-Roman inscriptions and writings express a pervasive interest in benefaction. These sources provide a critical starting point for interpreting

---

[8]Frederick W. Danker, "Benefactor," in *ABD* (1992), I: 670.
[9]Danker, *Benefactor*, 317.

biblical texts because they reflect the sociolinguistic context within which early Christians communicated.[10] Ignoring the language of Greco-Roman patronage removes the New Testament from its original contexts and risks distorting the intent of biblical writers. For this reason, these three chapters on theology discuss such terms and themes within their Greco-Roman social context. To understand key New Testament terms, we must first discern the everyday, common meaning of those terms (lest the terms serve as empty containers we fill with latter theological conversations).

And to clarify, the New Testament use of Greco-Roman benefaction language does not suggest Christianity is on par with ancient paganism. Rather, early Christians usurped common language to correct prevailing notions of patronage as well as express how Israel's God—the world's true patron—has acted through Jesus Christ for the benefit of all peoples. The Bible uses the language of patronage to subvert traditional views of reality.

## A TRINITARIAN THEOLOGY OF DIVINE PATRONAGE

The Trinitarian God confers benefactions in a complete and coordinated manner. Patronage positively informs the work of the Father, Son, and Holy Spirit.

God the Father is the creator and sustainer of all life (Genesis 1; Psalm 19; Acts 17:24-28; Revelation 4:9-11). God's life and grace indebts all people. We depend upon God's past and future gifts. Through the giving of his Son, God the Father displays his benevolence and offers deliverance for all peoples. His free gift is proclaimed and appropriated throughout the entire world, "to the praise of his glorious grace that he freely bestowed on us" (Ephesians 1:6). Though God shares his goodness with all people (Matthew 5:45; Acts 14:17), he becomes a personal patron to those clients who trust in his name and receive the gift of his Son. In prayer, every Christian has the privilege and assurance of direct access to God for specific help.[11] Nothing, not even death, can separate believers from the ongoing benevolence of God (Romans 8:32, 38).

---

[10]Danker, *Benefactor*, 29.
[11]David deSilva, *Honor, Patronage, Kinship & Purity: Unlocking New Testament Culture* (Downers Grove, IL: IVP Academic, 2000), 130-31.

Jesus Christ, the Son of God, brokers divine salvation. Jesus is the "one mediator between God and humankind" (1 Timothy 2:5; cf. John 14:6). Jerome Neyrey explains,

> Jesus bridges the heavenly and earthly worlds. God, the heavenly benefactor, has bestowed on us all benefaction through Jesus (e.g., Eph. 1.3-10). Similarly, all mortal prayers are made to God through Jesus, either petitionary prayers (Rom. 1.8; 7.25; 1 Cor. 15.57) or doxologies (Heb. 13.20-21; Jude 25). Jesus, then, mediates the heavenly patronage of God to us, even as he functions to mediate earthly petition and praise to the heavenly patron.[12]

Jesus has mediated divine favors since the dawn of creation (John 1:1-3; Colossians 1:15-20). But Jesus' ultimate benefaction was his voluntary death that ensures our rescue from sin, death, and evil. At the cross, Jesus incurred upon himself a great cost for our benefit, an act of unprecedented generosity (Romans 5:6-8; cf. 2 Corinthians 5:15; 8:9).[13] Because Jesus opened access to the Father by making purification of sins (Hebrews 1:3; 7:25; cf. Romans 8:34), we can now approach the Great Patron's throne of favors (Hebrews 4:16). Jesus' life is the work of "reconciliation," the brokering of new relationships. Moreover, Jesus is the ideal client who always honors the Father. His perfect obedience and loyalty as the Son allows him to bring other children into the divine family by extending his reputation to us (Hebrews 2:9-10).

The gift of the Holy Spirit is clear proof of God's generosity toward of all peoples. Early Christians were inclined to confine God's benefactions to ethnic Israel, but the radical gift of the Spirit symbolizes God's benevolence to all peoples. God's empowering presence is received by faith/faithfulness, regardless of any criteria of worth. The experience of the Holy Spirit is

> a gift from God that signifie[s] adoption into God's family (Gal 4:5-6), the fulfillment of the promise made to Abraham (Gal 3:14), the restoration of peace and favor with God (Rom 5:5), and a pledge of the future benefits God has prepared and will confer at the return of Jesus or after the believer's death (2 Cor 1:22; 5:5; Eph 1:13-14).[14]

---

[12]Neyrey, "God, Benefactor and Patron," 476.
[13]deSilva, *Honor, Patronage, Kinship & Purity*, 136.
[14]deSilva, *Honor, Patronage, Kinship & Purity*, 128-29.

The Holy Spirit assures Christians of God's future favors, "to the praise of his glory" (Ephesians 1:14). Moreover, the Holy Spirit himself distributes benefactions to the church. For example, "spiritual gifts" (Greek: *charisma*) are literally the "result of benevolence/favor." The Holy Spirit protects and secures believers from dangerous threats (Romans 8:2), as befitting for patrons. The Spirit also strengthens and empowers so we can obey God as loyal clients and declare his glorious benevolence to others.

## DIVINE PATRONAGE IN HISTORICAL THEOLOGY

Prominent theologians throughout church history—John Chrysostom, Basil of Caesarea, Jonathan Edwards, and George Müller—have spoken of God as a divine patron. Their writings offer instructive examples of a patronage theology, so we summarize their thoughts on the topic.

***John Chrysostom.*** John Chrysostom, an early church father and archbishop of Constantinople (353–407), was a prolific preacher. His eighty-eight homilies on the Gospel of John frequently use the concept and language of benefaction to explain key aspects of Christian theology.[15]

Chrysostom believed the ministry of Jesus was "to proclaim the common Benefactor of the world" (*Hom.* 17:2). Both the Holy Spirit and the cross of Jesus are a "benefaction" of God (*Hom.* 17:1). But despite God's benevolence, we humans insult our divine patron: "Consider what an insult is offered to your Benefactor, when He holds forth to you things above, and thou, making no great account of them chooses earth instead" (*Hom.* 31:5). Chrysostom summarizes the ideal relationships between God and humans in this way: "when such honor has been lavished upon us," we must repay "our so great Benefactor" (*Hom.* 11:2).

Chrysostom presents the blind man whom Jesus healed in John 9 as an exemplary model of grateful clientage. The man "was not so unfeeling as after such a benefit and charge to betray his Benefactor [i.e., Jesus]," but

---

[15]All citations from John Chrysostom, "Homilies on the Gospel of John," in *From Nicene and Post-Nicene Fathers,* ed. Philip Schaff, trans. Charles Marriott, rev. and ed. Kevin Knight, 1st ser., vol. 14 (Buffalo, NY: Christian Literature Publishing Co., 1889), cited from www.newadvent.org/fathers/240111.htm. For more about honor and shame in Chrysostom, see H. F. Stander, "Honour and Shame as Key Concepts in Chrysostom's Exegesis of the Gospel of John," *HTS Teologiese Studies / Theological Studies* 59, no. 3 (2003): 899-913.

was "seeking to attract and attach others to Him." He "proclaims his Bene-factor" with "words of great boldness and candor" (*Hom.* 38:2; cf. 57:1; 59:1). The blind man's loyal praise stands in contrast to Judas, "who having enjoyed ten thousand good things, repaid his Benefactor with the contrary" (*Hom.* 71:2). In talking about sin, Chrysostom says people have received kindness but often repay "their benefactors as though they had wronged them. Worse than wild beasts are [ingrates], like the devils" (*Hom.* 37:3).

***Basil of Caesarea.*** Basil of Caesarea (c. 330–379) was a Cappadocian Father and prominent bishop. During a severe famine, the rich were hoarding grain to profiteer. To motivate generosity, Basil explains our ob-ligation to the divine benefactor.

> From God comes everything beneficial . . . but human beings respond with a bitter disposition, misanthropy, and an unwillingness to share. Such charac-teristics are what this man offered back to his Benefactor. . . . O mortal, rec-ognize your Benefactor! Consider yourself, who you are, what resources have been entrusted to you, from whom you received them, and why you received more than others![16]

***Jonathan Edwards.*** Jonathan Edwards (1703–1758) was a Puritan pastor and Reformed theologian in early New England. His famous treatise *The End for Which God Created the World* speaks about God's glory in terms of a cosmic patron-client relationship. According to Edwards, God is of in-finite worth so must display his glory. God shares the knowledge of his glory with creatures, who delight and exult in his excellent perfections. God bestows the gift of his own glory, and humans magnify that glory. Salvation-history is patronage of the grandest scale. Edwards speaks often of God's "benevolence" or "beneficence"—as the good disposition in his nature to communicate his own glory. In the final sentence, Edwards concludes, "God, in glorifying the saints in heaven with eternal [joy], aims to satisfy his infinite grace or benevolence, by the bestowment of a good infinitely valuable."[17]

---

[16]St. Basil the Great, "I Will Tear Down My Barns," in *On Social Justice: St. Basil the Great*, trans. and ed. C. Paul Schroeder (Yonkers, NY: St. Vladimir's Seminar Press, 2009), 1-2.

[17]Jonathan Edwards, *The End for Which God Created the World*, par. 285. Cited from the full text re-printed in John Piper, *God's Passion for His Glory* (Wheaton, IL: Crossway, 1998), 251. Edward's

***George Müller.*** George Müller (1805–1898) was an evangelist and orphanage director in Bristol, England. In his classic autobiography *The Life of Trust*, Müller explains the key principle by which he operated his orphanage: "The Lord helping us, we do not mean to seek the *patronage of the world*; i.e., we never intend to ask unconverted persons of rank or wealth to countenance this Institution, because this, we consider, would be *dishonorable to the Lord.* In the name of our God we set up our banners, Ps. xx. 5; *he alone shall be our patron.*"[18] God provided miraculously for Müller's orphans over the course of many years. For Müller, divine patronage was not just a theological idea, but also a spiritual conviction expressed through a life of constant prayer and complete reliance upon God.

## THEOLOGICAL CORRECTIVES

The Bible and church fathers affirm the idea that God is a patron. But what does this mean to say, "God is a patron"? The word *patron* functions as a theological metaphor—a concept from human life that explains a spiritual reality about God. Like all metaphors in theology, the concept of "patron" has limitations. One reason is because our understanding of "patron" is derived from our interactions with human patrons who are sinful. These negative experiences taint our view of patronage. So while social patronage informs our view of God, we recognize that divine patronage significantly differs from human patronage in four key ways. The God of the Bible (1) foreordained the relationship, (2) expects exclusive allegiance, (3) prioritizes the relationship, and (4) preserves the permanent bond (see table 7.1).

First, human patronage is a voluntary arrangement. Clients choose which patron(s) they will follow and expect provisions from. Both sides freely choose to enter the relationship. But God foreordained his patronage

---

opponents suggested that God's self-interest would negate his "freeness of beneficence." That is, if God *must* save to preserve honor, then his gift is not voluntary. This would be problematic because it threatens to "diminish the creature's obligation to gratitude for communications of good received" (par. 121-23). But as Edwards argues, God extends his benevolence without constraints, so creatures do have an obligation of gratitude to God for his benefits.

[18]George Müller, *The Life of Trust* (New York: Thomas Y. Crowell and Company, 1898), 99, emphasis added.

before the foundations of the world (Ephesians 1:3-6; 2 Timothy 1:9). We are divinely elected to be the recipients of his favors. God initiates reconciliation long before human clients can make an overture or offer a token gift. Paul asked rhetorically, "Who has given a gift to him that he might be repaid?" (Romans 11:35 ESV). This relationship is not a client seeking a connection with someone higher, but the patron initiated with a gift of unparalleled benefit (John 3:16; Romans 3:22-26; 5:8).

Second, clients often toggle between multiple patrons (as long as those patrons are not competitors or enemies). The relationships are dynamic and fluid. In contrast, divine patronage requires exclusivity. The claim that God is Patron undercuts all other potential patrons. God's people must renounce rival patrons (e.g., Baal, Egypt, mammon, Caesar) and trust in God alone as the ultimate Patron.

Third, the motive of human patronage is rarely altruistic. People manipulate the system to squeeze as much benefit out of the other person. The arrangement can become overt exploitation. Clients and patrons may discard one another in the race for resources and personal advancement. In contrast, the motive of divine patronage is the relationship, not the benefits resulting from the arrangement. God himself *is* the gift; knowing God *is* the ultimate benefit; the relationship *is* the reward. God deserves our praise and allegiance because he is our Creator.

Fourth, human patronage has a limited time frame. Each side sustains the arrangement so long as it remains beneficial. The bond dissipates when either side does not reciprocate as expected. But divine patronage with God is permanent because God foreordained the relationship *from* and *for* eternity. Since the purpose of divine patronage is the relationship, an apparent lack of generosity from God does not sever the relationship. God is not a slot machine we walk away from when our luck runs cold. By his sovereign grace, God perseveres in the relationship until the end.[19]

---

[19]This does not deny the pastoral reality that some Christians turn from God because of a perceived lack of benefits from God (cf. Gal 5:4). Without delving into issues of election versus free will debate, we must note that people eternally chosen to be recipients of God's graces must intentionally sustain the divine-human patron-client relationship, as the authors of Hebrews and Revelation admonished early Christians.

| | HUMAN PATRONAGE | DIVINE PATRONAGE |
|---|---|---|
| Origin | Voluntary | God-initiated |
| Nature | Dynamic | Exclusive |
| Motive | Selfish | Relational |
| Scope | Provisional | Permanent |

**Table 7.1.** Human patronage vs. divine patronage

So in light of these differences can one still claim that God is a patron? Yes, but unlike any patron we have ever met.[20] Patronage is a biblical and helpful model for Christian theology, but the metaphor requires some clarification. A theology of divine patronage, when untethered from biblical truth, can deteriorate into an erroneous view of God and his salvation, as seen in "health-and-wealth theology." The prosperity gospel portrays God as the type of patron who automatically gives material blessings when we perform a certain way. Unchecked assumptions about patronage can warp our theology and cause a purely transactional exchange with God. A missionary researcher in Thailand observed this tendency among some Thai Christians. "When God blesses them then they return the favor by gratitude and loyalty (attend church, pray, etc.). When God does not bless them, then there could be the temptation to look for another patron, or else doubt whether God is such a good patron after all."[21] This is certainly a sub-biblical view of spiritual patronage.

---

[20]For a critique against the claim that patronage structured the divine-human relationship in Paul's thought, see David Downs, "Is God Paul's Patron? The Economy of Patronage in Pauline Theology," in *Engaging Economics: New Testament Scenarios and Early Christian Reception*, ed. Bruce Longenecker and Kelley Liebengood (Grand Rapids: Eerdmans, 2009), 129-56. Downs emphasizes the incongruence between human patronage (e.g., manipulation, limited good) and divine salvation, then concludes that God is not a patron in Paul's theology. However, such a distinction does not imply a *rejection* of social patronage, but a *transformation* of the cultural paradigm. Downs notes that the "terminology of the Roman patronage system" is absent in Paul's thought, but only allows the specific terms *patron*, *client*, and *patronage* to count as evidence. Finally, Downs notes that Paul speaks of God as a "father" *instead of* as a "patron." But this either-or reasoning is a false dichotomy (like saying a "wife" could not also be a "friend") for several reasons: parenting is one type of patron-client relationship; in both Ancient Near Eastern and Greco-Roman thought "father" was a common euphemism of patron; and the words patron (*patron*) and father (*patēr*) are derived from the same root word. Contra Downs's conclusions, patronage structures family relationships, and familial language describes patronage.
[21]Steve Taylor, "Gaps in Beliefs of Thai Christians," *EMQ* 37, no. 1 (Jan 2001): 79-80.

Divine patronage is not an entitlement program like a government welfare system, as some clients may expect. The biblical view of divine patronage is a relationship based on mutual loyalty and service. Viewing God as a patron is fundamentally about a reconciled relationship with our Creator—he confers grace and receives the honor.

## CONCLUSION

God's people have viewed God as the supreme Patron. He gives gifts and deserves the glory. This chapter examined the meaning and nature of divine patronage through New Testament linguistics, Trinitarian theology, and historical theology. The biblical presentation of God as a patron is not merely a theological declaration but a mutual relationship marked by reciprocity and divine praise, as Psalm 117 demonstrates:

> Praise the LORD, all you nations! Extol him, all you peoples!
> For great is his steadfast love toward us, and the faithfulness of the LORD endures forever.
> Praise the LORD!

# 8

# SIN AS INGRATITUDE

IN PATRONAGE RELATIONSHIPS, clients are morally obligated to express thankfulness and loyalty to patrons. The failure to properly reciprocate is disgraceful and immoral. This was a moral axiom for people in New Testament times. For example, the Roman philosopher Seneca (4 BC–AD 65) denounces ingratitude with utmost severity in his book about benefactions:

> There will always be killers, tyrants, thieves, adulterers, rapists, violators of religion, and traitors. But lower than all of these is the ungrateful man. . . . Treat it as the greatest crime. (*Ben.* 1.10.4)
>
> Someone who fails to return a benefit makes a bigger mistake. (*Ben.* 1.1.13)
>
> It is shameful, and everyone knows it, not to return the favor when benefits are conferred. (*Ben.* 3.1.1)
>
> Ingratitude is something to be avoided in itself because there is nothing that so effectually disrupts and destroys the harmony of the human race as this vice. (*Ben.* 4.18.1)

In the eyes of this New Testament contemporary, ingratitude is the worst crime, a horrific vice, a sin, and a universal disgrace. Greco-Roman philosophers such as Seneca illuminate the social thought world of early Christians.

The Bible's view of sin reflects a common feature of patronage relationships—ingratitude is sinful and evil. In a theological sense, God has showered benevolence upon his creation, but people have responded as ungrateful clients. Humans have been disloyal to the heavenly Patron. Sin in the Bible is not simply transgressing a legal code, but also despising and dishonoring God.[1] People fail offer to God thankfulness, praise, and honor

---

[1]For more, see Jayson Georges and Mark D. Baker, *Ministering in Honor-Shame Cultures: Biblical Foundations and Practical Essentials* (Downers Grove, IL: IVP Academic, 2016), 68-73.

as they ought. Sin, in essence, is acting as an unworthy and disloyal client towards God. Three portions of Scripture depict sin as ungratefulness towards God: David's adultery with Bathsheba, Paul indictment in Romans 1, and the exhortation to the Hebrews.

## DAVID'S ADULTERY

The story of David's adultery (2 Samuel 11) is straightforward—the king sleeps with a young wife, then gets away with murder (literally!). David senses no fault for his actions until God sends the prophet Nathan to rebuke him. Western readers easily misinterpret David's sin from a legal point of view. For example, study notes in the *ESV Study Bible* state that David was "standing above the law" and Nathan "intervene[s] in a legal matter."[2] Although David's envy, adultery, and murder did break several of the Ten Commandments, neither Nathan nor God mention any commandments in their rebuke.[3]

David's sinful actions were condemned not as a legal violation but a violation of patron-client expectations. His adultery rejected God's benevolence. This is sinful because it dishonors God. God rebukes David for despising his provisions.

> Thus says the LORD, the God of Israel: I anointed you king over Israel, and I rescued you from the hand of Saul; I gave you your master's house, and your master's wives into your bosom, and gave you the house of Israel and of Judah; and if that had been too little, I would have added as much more. Why have you despised the word of the LORD, to do what is evil in his sight? (2 Samuel 12:7-9)

We should interpret this passage in light of patronage. God first recounts his magnificent benevolence towards David: I anointed you king; I rescued you from Saul; I gave you his house and wives; I gave you the land of Israel. God has exalted a lowly shepherd boy to the royal throne. To emphasize his generosity, God emphatically offers, "If that had been too little, I would

---

[2]David Toshio Tsumura, "2 Sam 12:1-31 Notes," *The ESV Study Bible* (Wheaton, IL: Crossway, 2008), 560.

[3]This section on David's adultery is adapted from my "How David Sinned with Bathsheba," honor shame.com, April 27, 2016, http://honorshame.com/david-sinned-bathsheba.

have added as much more." God was faithful and eager to provide for David as a magnanimous patron. For this reason, God was right to expect gratefulness and loyalty from David.

But David "despised" the LORD. This means treating God as someone of low value and failing to rightly honor him as Patron.[4]

God says David despised "the word of the LORD." In this scenario God's "word" refers to the promise he made to David in 2 Samuel 7. God vowed to build a "house" (i.e., dynasty/empire) for David. God covenanted to David, "Your house and your kingdom will endure forever before me; your throne will be established forever" (2 Samuel 7:16 NIV). The "word of the Lord" is God's *covenant promise* to make David's kingdom great (see 2 Samuel 7:7-13 and 12:7). God had given his word to act as David's benefactor. By recounting all the benevolent favors he conferred upon David (2 Samuel 12:7), God emphasizes that he has kept his promises as patron.

By taking Bathsheba, David is turning from the provisions that God promised. David's actions functionally say that God cannot keep his promises nor provide as an honorable patron. David is a disloyal client to the generous patron, bypassing the patron-client relationship in order to access resources through other channels. Rejecting God's provisions diminishes his benevolence. This is how David's actions were "evil in God's eyes," and "utterly scorned the LORD" (2 Samuel 12:14). The rebuke from Nathan emphasizes how David violated God's honor as his patron.

David's sinful adultery with Bathsheba reflects an Old Testament motif—Yahweh greatly blessed Israel, yet they turn to other sources for benefits. This sin of ungratefulness and disloyalty dishonors God.

## ROMANS 1

The argument of Romans opens with a lengthy explanation of the human problem of sin. In Romans 1:18-32, Paul depicts human sin as ungratefulness and dishonor towards God. People have been ungrateful clients in their

---

[4]David deSilva, "Honor and Shame," in *Dictionary of the Pentateuch* (Downers Grove, IL: InterVarsity Press, 2003), 435

relationships with God, our heavenly Patron. I paraphrase Romans 1:18-32 below to highlight its patron-client dynamics.[5]

People have dishonored God by losing sight of their rightful position in the world. So now, he is avenging those insults against his name, as I'll explain.

All people have experienced God's gracious benefactions and know how glorious he truly is. It's been obvious to them! Although people know the glories of God the Creator, they simply have not honored him as they ought. When humans fail to reciprocate with gratitude, God loses face. Over time, their minds became incapable of discerning what (and who!) deserved honor. They've lost all sense of shame.

So instead of attributing glory to their benevolent Creator, they esteem the things he created (like Israel worshipping the golden calf at Sinai). So God lets them chase their vainglories. People only became more disgusting as humans, dishonoring their own bodies. This happens as people invert the social hierarchy and disrespect the Patron on top.

However, the truth remains—God himself is our Creator and Patron, and he alone deserves all our praise and honors! When people misattribute honor, their disgraceful vainglories become all-consuming. For example, they pursue intimacy and connection in all the wrong places. Their perverse sexual actions with one another exacerbate their disgrace and isolation.

Without any sense of shame before God, they become destructive towards other people.

They destroy their own community in such wicked ways. Their hearts are full of jealousy and animosity against neighbors. They spread gossip, slander others, belittle God, exalt themselves, take pride in their status over others, do vicious things, and humiliate their own parents.

They know that God will cut off and banish such people. But still, they keep doing the same shameful and divisive things. And even worse, they perpetuate this entire cycle of disgrace by esteeming others who do likewise.

Paul explains human sin as dishonoring ungratefulness towards God. All peoples, both Jews and Gentiles, owe their Creator thanks and praise (cf. Romans 11:35-36). "It is precisely here, however that humanity has failed. Neither Gentile nor Jew returned to God the reverence and service God merited but went so far as to insult God through blatant disobedience

---

[5]This dynamic paraphrase highlights patronal aspects of Paul's theology on sin. The linguistic and theological assumptions behind this passage are explained in other sections throughout the book.

(Romans 1:18-24)."[6] Romans 1–3 depicts sin as human ingratitude and God as the dishonored benefactor.

## HEBREWS

David deSilva uses insights from social anthropology to interpret the book of Hebrews.[7] He explains how Hebrews draws on the ideology of patronage to admonish believers who were facing persecution. According to his interpretation of Hebrews, believers have God's assurance of future inheritance and so "must resist the danger to shrink back (10:39) in the face of society's rejection, insult, and abuse. For . . . such a shrinking back would be an outrage to God, their benefactor and parent."[8] In a hostile world, Christians approach the throne of divine favors, trusting that God will reliably bring salvation. Believers must encourage "one another to seek honor in terms of what God requires of God's clients."[9] Two passages in Hebrews caution believers against becoming disloyal clients: Hebrews 3:7-19 and Hebrews 6:4-8.

In Hebrews 3, the wilderness generation that refused to enter Canaan is a negative example of disloyal clients (Hebrews 3:7-9; cf. Numbers 14; Psalm 95). Those Israelites failed "to appreciate God's sufficiency as patron, provoked God to anger, thereby losing the benefits God promised them—a thing highly to be feared."[10] Their lack of faith "was an affront to their benefactor—a vote of no confidence."[11] Israel had challenged God's honor and sufficiency as a patron. So God responded, "How long will this people despise me? And how long will they refuse to believe in me, in spite of all the signs that I have done among them?" (Numbers 14:11). God has

---

[6]David deSilva, *Honor, Patronage, Kinship & Purity: Unlocking New Testament Culture* (Downers Grove, IL: IVP Academic, 2000), 127.

[7]David deSilva, "Despising Shame: A Cultural-Anthropological Investigation of the Epistle to the Hebrews," *JBL* 113, no. 3 (September 1994): 439-61; *Despising Shame: Honor Discourse and Community Maintenance in the Epistle to the Hebrews* (Atlanta: Scholars Press, 1995); "Hebrews 6:4-8: A Socio-Rhetorical Investigation (Part 1)," *Tyndale Bulletin* 50, no. 1 (1999): 33-57; "Hebrews 6:4-8: A Socio-Rhetorical Investigation (Part 2)," *Tyndale Bulletin* 50, no. 2 (1999): 225-35; *The Letter to the Hebrews in Social-Scientific Perspective* (Eugene, OR: Cascade Books, 2012).

[8]deSilva, *Despising Shame*, 455.

[9]deSilva, *Despising Shame*, 455.

[10]deSilva, *Despising Shame*, 452.

[11]deSilva, *Despising Shame*, 453.

conferred many favors, but Israel refuses to trust him for future deliverance. This, in effect, diminishes God's name and glory as their patron.

The sin of the wilderness generation serves as a warning to Christians facing opposition (Hebrews 3:14-19). Believers are to act with faith and belief, which "is based on the recognition of the honor and trustworthiness of God. Thus to act without faith is not merely to be unreliable, or to be disobedient, but involves an affront to God, whose honor is impugned by lack of faith."[12] In Hebrews, "unbelief" (Gr: *apistia*) is being an untrustworthy client of the benevolent God.

Hebrews 6:4-6 also uses the paradigm of patronage to condemn sinful behavior and induce repentance. The passage reads,

> For it is impossible to restore again to repentance those who have once been enlightened, and have tasted the heavenly gift, and have shared in the Holy Spirit, and have tasted the goodness of the word of God and the powers of the age to come, and then have fallen away, since on their own they are crucifying again the Son of God and are holding him up to contempt.

This passage speaks about "people who have received God's gifts, who have been benefited by God's generosity."[13] They have "tasted the heavenly gift," a patronage favor. They have also tasted the "goodness" and "powers" of God, which refers to their experience of divine provision (cf. Psalm 34). In sum, "The subjects of 6:4-5 are clearly described in terms of the reception of benefits. They have been graced by God in this variety of ways, being granted great privileges and promises, as well as proofs of their patron's good will toward them."[14] The author of Hebrews does not explain whether these people were "saved" or "unsaved" (as theologians debate) but identifies them foremost as beneficiaries of God's favor.

Sadly, these people have "fallen away" from God's benevolence. They turned away from fellow believers and returned to the world for approval and favors. In other words, they have neglected a great salvation (Hebrews 2:3) and failed to obtain the gift of God (Hebrews 12:15). Trampling upon the gift of God's salvation is tantamount to re-crucifying God's son

---

[12]deSilva, *Despising Shame*, 453 n. 42.
[13]deSilva, "Hebrews 6 (Part 1)," 1999, 44.
[14]deSilva, "Hebrews 6 (Part 1)," 1999, 47.

and "subjecting him to public disgrace" (Hebrews 6:6 NIV). "In their slight regard for God's gifts and promises, they have made the vicious response of offering insult to their benefactor."[15] In Hebrews, Christians must not forgo the promises and gifts of God in order to minimize social tensions. Such behavior proves one is an unworthy client in the eyes of God.

## THEOLOGICAL IMPLICATIONS

Old Testament and New Testament authors interpret sin through the conceptual metaphor of patronage. Sin involves being an ungrateful and unthankful client who dishonors the generous patron, God. We conclude with several implications of this point.

First, the idea of sin as bad clientage echoes a prominent Old Testament motif—spiritual forgetfulness. Israel, like all people, suffered from "soteriological amnesia." The human mind easily forgets the benefits and blessings of God's salvation. The sinful heart often responds to God's favor with complaining ("This is not a *good* gift!") and anxiety ("What about tomorrow?"). Ungratefulness demeans God's generosity, trustworthiness, and honor. For this reason, many Psalms recount God's salvation and faithfulness (cf. Psalms 78, 105, and 106). God's people must not forget his favors. To keep from becoming ungrateful clients before God, we must heed Psalm 103:2 (emphasis added): "Bless the LORD, O my soul, and *do not forget all his benefits*."

Second, the dynamics of patronage illuminate the nature of God's wrath and anger. Western theology explains God's wrath as a legal mandate— punishment is the just retribution of a law-abiding God. But the wrath of God also involves "the anger of a slighted benefactor, whose favor is met not with gratitude but with rejection and affront in the form of idolatrous worship or in the form of violence against God's loyal clients."[16] In patronage cultures, insults to one's reputation merit opprobrium and exclusion from future favor. For example, Dio Chrysostom said, "Those who insult their benefactors will by nobody be esteemed to deserve a favour" (*Or.* 31.65). Bad clients deserve punishment.

---

[15]deSilva, "Hebrews 6 (Part 1)," 1999, 48.

[16]David deSilva, *The Hope of Glory: Honor Discourse and New Testament Interpretation* (Collegeville, MN: The Liturgical Press, 1999), 98.

Hebrews 6 compares the ingrates who re-crucify and shame God's son to soil that receives rain in vain—"If it produces thorns and thistles, it is worthless and on the verge of being cursed; its end is to be burned over" (Hebrews 6:8). People who receive blessings and return nothing bring upon themselves a shameful curse and destruction. Such divine wrath against ungrateful sinners preserves God's preeminent honor.

Third, the concept of sin as ingratitude and disloyal clientage has precedent in church history. One example is the Puritan preacher Thomas Watson (c. 1620–1686), who warned about the sinfulness of spiritual ingratitude in his book *The Doctrine of Repentance*.

> In sin there is odious ingratitude. God has fed you, O sinner, with angels' food. He has crowned you with a variety of mercies, yet you continue in sin? As David said of Nabal: "in vain I have protected this man's sheep" (1 Sam 25.21). Likewise in vain has God done so much for the sinner. All God's mercies may upbraid, even accuse the ungrateful person. God may say he gave you wit, health, riches, and you employed all these against him.[17]
>
> In every sin there is much unthankfulness, and that is a matter of shame. The one who is upbraided with ingratitude will blush. . . . We have had the finest of the wheat; we have been fed with angels' food. The golden oil of divine blessing has run down on us from the head of our heavenly Aaron. And to abuse the kindness of so good a God, how this may make us ashamed! . . . How unworthy it is to contract the disease of pride and luxury from the perfume of God's mercy; to requite evil for good; to kick against our feeder (Deut 32.15); to make an arrow of God's mercies and shoot it at him; to wound him with his own blessing! O horrid ingratitude! Will not this dye our faces a deep scarlet? Unthankfulness is a sin so great that God himself stands amazed at it: "Hear, O heavens, and give ear, O earth: I have nourished and brought up children, and they have rebelled against me" (Isa 1.2).[18]

As clients in the divine-human relationship, we are called to honor and praise God for all his benefits. In such a relational context, unthankfulness blasphemes the honorable and loving generosity of God. For this reason, Scripture depicts sin as being an unworthy and disloyal client towards God.

---

[17]Thomas Watson, *The Doctrine of Repentance*, modernized and ed. William Gross (1668; Carlisle, PA: Banner of Truth Trust, 2011), 52, www.onthewing.org/user/Watson%20-%20Repentance%20-%20 Modern.pdf.

[18]Watson, *Doctrine of Repentance*, 17.

# 9

# SALVATION AS PATRONAGE

GOD IS THE DIVINE PATRON WHO DESERVES PRAISE, but ungrateful human clients have insulted his honor. Sin separates people from God's benevolence. But God has acted through Jesus to repair his honor and reconstitute the patron-client relationship with his creation. To explain this divine salvation, New Testament authors use the language and concepts of patronage. Biblical salvation follows the paradigm of patronage—humans receive God's benevolent gift(s), and God gets praise and loyalty from his grateful clients.[1]

The key words that early Christians used to explain divine salvation came from the social world of patronage and benefaction.[2] Contemporary theology must account for the fact that key New Testament words originally came from the social world of patronage. Paul and other apostles certainly knew that the Greco-Roman converts who received their letters would interpret their message in light of that shared cultural meaning. To impose theological paradigms from church history or semantic meaning from English words upon first-century texts is exegetically irresponsible, if not culturally imperialistic. Key theological concepts and terms must be situated in their first-century meaning. A soteriology framed by patronage

---

[1]Jayson Georges and Mark D. Baker, *Ministering in Honor-Shame Cultures: Biblical Foundations and Practical Essentials* (Downers Grove, IL: IVP Academic, 2016), 198.

[2]Readers of English translations of the Bible can misinterpret key concepts because English words reflect the values of a modern, democratic, technological, individualistic culture. Moreover, the meaning of key theology terms in English has been shaped by centuries of theological conversations (especially the Reformation). For example, the words of *salvation* and *grace* in Western theology connote a legal transaction in the heavenly realms—i.e., "forgiveness of sins." And *faith* often means cognitive acceptance of that forgiveness. However, the Greek terms carried different connotations in the social world of the New Testament. They were most at home in the reciprocal relationships of sociopolitical economics.

does not invalidate historical Christian theology but provides a broader framework for interpreting and applying biblical theology.

Reciprocity was an integral part of ancient Jewish and Greco-Roman religion. The God-human relationship was based on gift-reciprocity. Gods were acknowledged as benefactors who distributed favors, while humans returned prayers and gifts in exchange.[3] No human could fully repay the gods and equalize the relationship, so they instead offered symbolic gifts to repay the divine benevolence.[4] In the patronage ideology, worship and praise towards benefactors are a common expression of a client's gratitude. The ethos and language of patronage characterized first-century religious practice, both Jewish and pagan.

The ancient concept of "salvation" had to do more with earthly bene-factions like health and military liberation (from either gods or humans) than eternal life for the soul.[5] Ben Witherington explains, "The 'salvation' most ancients looked for was salvation from disease, disaster, or death in this life."[6] In ancient documents and inscriptions, the word *sōtēr* ("savior") refers to benefactors and *sōtēria* ("salvation") connotes pa-tronage. Danker states, "The noun *soter* and cognates refer to the general manifestation of generous concern for the well-being of others, with the denotation of rescue from perilous circumstances," and savior is "the practical equivalent of *euergetes* [benefactor], with which it is frequently paired."[7] The notion of patronage structured first-century concepts of religion and "salvation."

---

[3]John Barclay, *Paul and the Gift* (Grand Rapids: Eerdmans, 2015), 27.

[4]Jonathan Marshall, *Jesus, Patrons, and Benefactors: Roman Palestine and the Gospel of Luke* (Eugene, OR: Wipf & Stock, 2015), 29-31.

[5]Ramsay MacMullen, *Paganism in the Roman Empire* (New Haven, CT: Yale University Press, 1983), 49.

[6]Ben Witherington, *Conflict and Community in Corinth: Socio-Rhetorical Commentary on 1 and 2 Corinthians* (Grand Rapids: Eerdmans, 1995), 821.

[7]Frederick W. Danker, *Benefactor: Epigraphic Study of a Greco-Roman and New Testament Semantic Field* (St. Louis, MO: Clayton Publishing House, 1982), 324. The connection between "salvation" and benefaction is apparent in Acts 4:12. Peter speaks of the *sōtēria* ("salvation") that is available only through the name of Jesus. In the story, "salvation" naturally refers to the healing of the crippled beggar at Solomon's Portico (Acts 3), which Peter describes as an "*euergesia* [lit. "benefaction"] done to some-one who was sick" (Acts 4:9). According to Peter, the salvation through Jesus was the benefaction of healing. *Sōtēria* in Acts 4:12 most certainly means more than just a "benefaction of healing," but this is nevertheless the foundational element for Peter and his audience in that story.

New Testament theology appropriates the Greco-Roman language for patronage to explain biblical salvation as divine patronage and believers' response as loyal clientage. This chapter explains the soteriological concepts of "grace," "faith," and "repentance" through their original social context of patronage. To clarify, this chapter does not seek merely to "contextualize" biblical salvation for contemporary contexts but explains soteriology in light of the New Testament's original, sociocultural contexts of patronage (which happens to resemble Majority World cultures more than modern, Western cultures). Then to understand how Jesus' death secures divine patronage, the final section examines Anselm's atonement theory.

## GRACE

The Greek word *charis* ("grace") comes from the ancient social context of patronage and benefaction.[8] In the social world of the New Testament, *grace* functioned as sociopolitical terminology of reciprocal exchange.[9] One scholar says *charis* was "the central leitmotif of the Hellenistic reciprocity system" throughout the Greco-Roman world.[10] The *Greek-English Lexicon of the NT* explains the word *grace* was "almost a technical term in the reciprocity-oriented word dominated by Hellenic influence as well as by the Semitic sense of social obligation expressed in the term *hesed*."[11] The context of *charis* was social reciprocity and patronage, not personal spirituality or systematic theology as in contemporary Christianity. Some scholars even question whether the English word "grace" is an accurate translation of *charis*, as it has become a theological shibboleth for some Christians today.[12]

---

[8]David deSilva, *Honor, Patronage, Kinship & Purity: Unlocking New Testament Culture* (Downers Grove, IL: IVP Academic, 2000), 104.

[9]Zeba A. Crook, *Reconceptualising Conversion: Patronage, Loyalty, and Conversion in the Religions of the Ancient Mediterranean* (New York: De Gruyter, 2004), 141. See also, James Harrison, *Paul's Language of Grace in Its Graeco-Roman Context* (Tübingen: Mohr Siebeck, 2003).

[10]James Harrison, *Paul's Language of Grace in Its Graeco-Roman Context* (Tübingen: Mohr Siebeck, 2003), 2.

[11]*BDAG, s.v.*

[12]Crook, *Reconceptualising Conversion*, 147, says, "Unfortunately, a term like 'grace' is so loaded with modern theological implications and post-Reformation overtones that unless modern theological application is the goal, such a translation risks being thoroughly meaningless."

In Greco-Roman books about reciprocity and patronage, the word *charis* entails three aspects of reciprocal exchanges.[13] "First, *grace* was used to refer to the willingness of a patron to grant some benefit to another person."[14] This refers to a patron's generous disposition or benevolence. Such kindness was an esteemed moral virtue. The New Testament says, "The *grace* of God was upon him [Jesus]" (Luke 2:40), and "Let us therefore approach the throne of *grace* with boldness, so that we may receive mercy and find *grace*" (Hebrews 4:16).

The word *charis* also "carries a second sense, often being used to denote the gift itself, that is, the result of the giver's beneficent feelings."[15] This *grace* is the actual "benefit," "favor," or "gift." *Charis* is the concrete expression to a patron's goodwill toward a client. *Charis* is the gift that inaugurated a relationship of reciprocity and dependence.[16] Paul says in 1 Corinthians 16:3, "I will send any whom you approve with letters to take your gift [*charin*] to Jerusalem." James says that God gives greater benefaction to the humble (see James 4:6).[17]

Finally, "*grace*" occasionally describes the recipient's response to a gift. The word refers to the client's "gratitude" and "thankfulness," the acknowledgement of benefaction. Recipients of *charis* (benefaction) must return *charis* (gratitude) to fulfill their social debt (lest they become dis-*graced*). So, for example, Christians give *charis* to God: "Thanks [*charis*] be to God through Jesus Christ our Lord!" (Romans 7:25; cf. 6:17; 1 Timothy 1:12). Hebrews 12:28 instructs, "Therefore *let us be grateful* [*exōmen charin*] for receiving a kingdom that cannot be shaken" (ESV, italics added).

The threefold meaning of *charis*—generosity, gift, and gratitude—underscores how *grace* was the social bond uniting people in a reciprocal relationship. In summary, *grace* is gift-giving benefaction, the relational giving and repaying of favors.

---

[13]deSilva, *Honor, Patronage, Kinship & Purity*, 104-6. This taxonomy is corroborated by Zeba A. Crook, *Reconceptualising Conversion*, 132-50; Harrison, *Paul's Language of Grace in Its Graeco-Roman Context*; *BDAG*, *s.v.* The word *charis* can also mean "pleasing/beautiful" (cf. Lk 4:22), but this use is rare and unrelated to patronage.

[14]deSilva, *Honor, Patronage, Kinship & Purity*, 104.

[15]deSilva, *Honor, Patronage, Kinship & Purity*, 104.

[16]Crook, *Reconceptualising Conversion*, 135.

[17]God's benefaction (*charis*) includes: justification (Rom 3:24), peace (Rom 5:1-2), righteousness (Rom 5:17), holiness (2 Cor 1:12), joy and liberality (2 Cor 8:1) and richness (2 Cor 8:9).

In the New Testament world, the term *grace* does not simply mean the forgiveness of sin before a judge but rather God's benefaction and gifts, which certainly include the gift of legal forgiveness of sin but also much more, including relationship, protection, care, generosity, help, empowerment, loyalty, trust and praise.[18]

Early Christians, socialized in the matrix of patronage, would have understood God's *grace* as the basis of a new relationship with mutual expectations.

In the New Testament, *charis* invokes the framework of patronage to explain salvation in Christ. However, the Christ-event subversively redefines key elements of the reciprocal relationship between God and humans. Compared to Jewish and Greco-Roman society, New Testament authors portray God's *charis* in Jesus Christ as distinctly *incongruous*—the recipients of God's gift are not worthy or deserving of God's grace. The extravagance of the gift does not proportionately match the worthiness of the elect. Such radical incongruity between the giver's generosity and the recipients' unworthiness is the defining characteristic of God's *charis*. God's grace is unconditional because it does not have any prior conditions, not because it is entirely free of any subsequent expectation.[19] As Harvard Old Testament professor Jon Levenson says, "God does not give his gifts anonymously. There is a personal God who gives gifts, and recipients have a new relationship."[20]

In ancient societies, favors were granted on the basis of worth. Ethnic Israelites thought only those who observed Torah deserved God's beneficence. In first-century Jewish theology and Greco-Roman life, *charis* was merited, given on the basis of worthiness. First-century people imagined that God's generosity "would be limited to those who were qualified, in one way or another, for his gifts. But Paul announces the divine gift given without regard to worth."[21] Such unworthiness is the defining feature of biblical *charis*.

---

[18]Richard Yakoub, "The Amazingly Generous God" (unpublished paper, Lebanon, 2016), 11. Used with permission from author.

[19]John Barclay's *Paul and the Gift* sets forth the various perfections of grace in these terms.

[20]Jon Levenson, "The Love of God," OnScript.com, December 26, 2017, onscript.study/podcast /episode-12-jon-d-levenson-the-love-of-god/.

[21]John Barclay, "The Meaning of God's Grace," *HonorShame.com,* January 20, 2016, honorshame.com /the-meaning-of-gods-grace/.

God's patronage ignores all prior notions of status. The benevolent salvation (*charis*) of God disregards all cultural and ethnic systems of worth (Galatians 3:28). People living under the power of sin have neglected all expectations of loyalty, making them unworthy of benevolence. But God gives his sacrificial gift *in*congruously to *un*worthy sinners, even to enemies like Saul of Tarsus bent on undermining God's generosity towards "outsiders" (cf. 1 Corinthians 15:9-10; Galatians 1:13-15; Ephesians 3:7-8). God gives to enemies what a virtuous person hardly shares with a friend (Romans 5:6-11). The Creator elects those who are *un*worthy of his gifts to accentuate the supremacy of his benevolence (1 Corinthians 1:26-31). Titus 3:3-5 explains the incongruity of divine grace: "For we ourselves were once foolish, disobedient, led astray, slaves to various passions and pleasures, passing our days in malice and envy, despicable, hating one another. But when the goodness and loving kindness of God our Savior appeared, he saved us." Even despite our unworthiness as clients, God extends *charis* to us.

In New Testament writings, God's *charis* has a clear purpose—God's own honor. The generous gift of God enhances his glory by stimulating thanks and moral virtue (Romans 8:12, 2 Corinthians 5:15).[22] Our salvation is "so that grace, as it extends to more and more people, may increase thanksgiving, to the glory of God" (2 Corinthians 4:15). In other words, "Thanks be to God for his indescribable gift!" (2 Corinthians 9:15). By using the language of *charis*, New Testament authors explain salvation in Christ through the cultural prism of patronage.

## FAITH

The Greek word *pistis* is also "very much at home in patron-client and friendship relationships."[23] *Pistis* refers to a person's trustworthiness and dependability in a relationship. In normal biblical usage, *pistis* "is a quality of firmness, fidelity, and reliability."[24] Both patrons and clients must demonstrate this *pistis*: reliable patrons kept their promises to provide, and

---

[22]For more on how the intended effects of God's gift in the Christian life, see deSilva, *Honor, Patronage, Kinship & Purity*, 145-48.

[23]deSilva, *Honor, Patronage, Kinship & Purity*, 115.

[24]Barnabas Lindars, *The Theology of the Letter to the Hebrews* (New York: Cambridge University Press, 1991), 109.

reliable clients expressed loyalty and gratitude.[25] This mirrors the Old Testament idea of faith, which was "a covenantal concept that describes the dynamic, mutual relationship between God and his people: an affirmation in word and deed of Israel's covenant obligations to God, who is faithful and loyal to his covenant with his people Israel."[26] Israel's "faith" was not a set of cognitive ideas *about* God but an embodied allegiance *to* God as their sovereign. In this view, the opposite of faith/faithfulness would be treason and disloyalty (not intellectual doubt or atheism).[27]

Most English Bibles translate this word *pistis* as "faith" and "belief," words that suggest a private disposition or ideological opinion. In English, the word "faith" refers to personal religion, so its meaning lacks the sense of relational obligation or covenantal bond that was often the dominant characteristic of *pistis*.[28] The word *pistis* is not primarily internal emotions or cognitive assent, but a sense of covenant loyalty and allegiance. For this reason, the concepts "faithfulness," "loyalty," and "allegiance" may better capture the biblical notion of *pistis*.[29]

People in honor-shame cultures place a high value on relational loyalty and commitment to a group leader. Families are close knit kinship groups where individual members are expected to remain faithful to the group. One example of this is Asian families. Young adults are expected to choose a career that reflects positively on their parents, there is a strong sense of familial loyalty, and children's obedience brings honor to their parents. This strongly relational notion of group loyalty best approximates the meaning of *pistis*, not the Western sense of "my personal faith."

In the Greco-Roman world, *pistis* refers to the type of loyalty "found in the positive actions that a client takes to protect his patron from enemies,

---

[25]deSilva, *Honor, Patronage, Kinship & Purity*, 115.

[26]Peter Enns, "Honor and Shame," in *Dictionary of the Old Testament: Historical Books*, ed. Bill Arnold and H. Williamson (Downers Grove, IL: IVP Academic, 2005), 296-300.

[27]This section about faith adapts my article, "Talking About Faith in Non-Western Contexts," *Modern Reformation* 26:4 (2017), www.whitehorseinn.org/article/talking-about-faith-in-non-western-contexts.

[28]Crook, *Reconceptualising Conversion*, 210.

[29]*Pistis* occasionally refers to "that which is believed" (e.g. Acts 6:7). The conversation here discusses the more common usage denoting one's response to Jesus. The phrase *pistis Christou* can be translated as "faith in Christ" (objective genitive) or "faithfulness of Christ" (subjective genitive). While *pistis* is the action of both Christ and the believer, we only discuss the latter in this section on conversion. For more, see Mark D. Baker, *Religious No More* (Downers Grove, IL: InterVarsity Press, 1999), 104-7.

that he takes to increase the honour and public reputation of his patron, and that he takes simply to reflect well on his patron."[30] This loyalty is a publicly demonstrated allegiance to the group and its leader. "*Pistis* is a commitment to remain faithful to the relational covenant, and purposefully seeks to promote the honor of a superior via obedience to their authority."[31] For example, the Roman philosopher Dio Chrysostom explains that a king's ability to rule and control depended upon the *pistis* of his friends, not money, armies, or laws.[32] This *pistis* does not refer to the religious beliefs of the king's client but their sociopolitical allegiance and concrete loyalty.

This sense of loyalty is evident in the New Testament's use of *pistis*. For example, servants are "described as *pistis*, in the sense of faithful, or trust-worthy (Mt 24:45; 25:21; 1 Cor 4:2).[33] The apostle Paul defines the Christian life as "living by faith," a reality that is "expressed in new patterns of loyalty and behavior."[34] The phrase "justified by faith" (Romans 3:21-31; Galatians 2:16-20) was a shorthand declaration about membership into God's covenant/client community—the beneficiaries of God's favors.[35] According to Paul, faithfulness or loyalty to God's new king, not observing Torah or other ethnic distinctions, declares a person in God's family (i.e., "justified"). "Justification by faith" dismantled the Judaizers' socially constructed value system that privileged Torah-observers as worthy (i.e., "righteous") beneficiaries of divine gifts.

In Revelation, *pistis* refers to a person's relational fidelity more than cerebral thoughts. One scholar translates Revelation 2:13 as, "You did not deny your loyalty to me even in the time of Antipas, who was steadfast in declaring his loyalty to me that he was put to death among you."[36] Early Christians distinguished themselves from pagan neighbors by giving

---

[30] Crook, *Reconceptualising Conversion*, 208.
[31] Georges and Baker, *Ministering in Honor-Shame Cultures*, 198.
[32] 3 *Regn.* 86, 88; referenced from Crook, *Reconceptualising Conversion*, 211.
[33] Crook, *Reconceptualising Conversion*, 212.
[34] Barclay, *Paul and the Gift*, 444.
[35] Georges and Baker, *Ministering in Honor-Shame Cultures*, 178; James D. G. Dunn, *Theology of Paul the Apostle* (Grand Rapids: Eerdmans, 1998), 334-98; Robert Jewett, "Honor and Shame in the Argument of Romans," in *Putting Body and Soul Together: Essays in Honor of Robin Scroggs*, ed. Graydon F. Snyder, Virginia Wiles, and Alexandra Brown (Valley Forge, PA: Trinity Press International, 1997), 270.
[36] William Barclay, *The New Testament: A New Translation* (London: Collins, 1968).

undivided loyalty (*pistis*) to Christ instead of Roman leaders or pagan gods. Such steadfast faithfulness enhances God's name and renown by demonstrating allegiance, even when it prompts persecution.

Clients also display *pistis* by trusting in the goodwill and ability of their patrons. Our *pistis* is bold confidence in God's future benefaction—"And without faith [*pisteōs*] it is impossible to please God, for whoever would approach him must believe [*pisteusai*] that he exists and that he rewards those who seek him" (Hebrews 11:6). *Pistis* is the confident expectation of God's future benefits. In sum, having *pistis* as a client involves being both trustworthy and trusting.

The notion of loyalty is also inherent in the word *lord*. Western Christianity speaks of Jesus as "my personal Lord," as though there is no public or social implication to faith in Christ. But for early Christians, the confession "Jesus is Lord" declared Jesus' sovereign provision and their allegiance to him. Vinoth Ramachandra notes, "The earliest Christian profession, 'Jesus is Lord,' was never merely a statement of personal devotion but a claim to universal validity. Christian mission made sense only on the premise that the crucified Jesus has been enthroned as the true Lord of the whole world, and thus claiming allegiance of the whole world."[37] Jesus' lordship means global patronage—he is the king who provides benevolent salvation to those committed to his reign. The confession "Jesus is Lord" declares our allegiance and subverts all claims of false patronage. In our relationship with the Lord, *pistis* is the loyalty of a faithful client.

The New Testament words *sōtēria, charis,* and *pistis* each come from the ancient social world of patronage. However, the common English translations of "salvation," "grace," and "faith" carry subtly different meanings than their Greek counterparts. This impacts the meaning of Ephesians 2:8: "For by *grace* you have been *saved* through *faith.*" A paraphrase with fresh terminology might better capture Paul's original intent: "God's generous benevolence has rescued you from peril, by means of steadfast loyalty to the relationship."[38]

---

[37]Vinoth Ramachandra, *The Recovery of Mission: Beyond the Pluralist Paradigm* (Eugene, OR: Wipf & Stock, 2002), 226.
[38]This paraphrase is admittedly choppy because English, unlike Majority World languages, lacks extensive vocabulary for reciprocal relationships.

## CONVERSION AND REPENTANCE

Patronage also affects the meanings of conversion and repentance. In Jesus' day, various Jewish groups advanced competing ideologies for how Jews should be worthy clients and thus secure divine patronage. Jesus summons his Jewish kinsmen to turn away from those warped approaches for securing benefits and instead give their allegiance to him (Mark 1:15). Those who associate with Jesus truly experience the salvation of God's reign. Repentance, in essence, is the transfer of one's allegiance from false patrons to the true Patron, a change in patronal relationships.

Conversion in the Western experience is typically a "personal religious experience" or "psychological enlightenment." In *Reconceptualising Conversion*, Zeba Crook explains how conversion in collectivistic contexts is "a change in patronal relationship" which "entails pledges of loyalty."[39] Ancient recipients of benefaction used common language to describe their newly formed patron-client relationships, such as: the patron's "call" to the client, the language of *charis*, the comparison of the client's life before and after, and praise for the patron.[40] Paul uses this language of benefaction when describing his own conversion—God "called" him by *charis*, the chief sinner became God's apostle for God's glory (1 Corinthians 15:8-10; Galatians 1:13-17; Philippians 3:4-11). Paul portrayed his own calling as a renewed patronage relationship with God.

The nature of idolatry sheds light on the biblical meaning of repentance. Idols are in essence false patrons; they promise benefactions and demand loyalties. Idols are things we hope in for security and provision. For ancient Israel, idolatry meant hoping in Egypt, Baal, or their own military to provide what God had promised. People in the contemporary world still seek blessings and protection through alternative means—e.g., deceased ancestors, an educational degree, and politicians with great promises. We must repent of those idols and transfer our loyalties to Jesus, the divine patron and heavenly provider.

Notions of patronage also affect conversion at the social level, as I learned while ministering in Central Asia. Asifa was born into a Muslim

---

[39]Crook, *Reconceptualising Conversion*, 250.
[40]Crook, *Reconceptualising Conversion*, 92.

family. While studying in university, she began to follow Jesus. Her Muslim family members harassed, shamed, and threatened her. They accused Asifa of converting for a financial payment. Her family asked, "How much did the Christians pay you?" In her parent's eyes, Asifa was an ungrateful child. She was turning her back on her parents after a lifetime of provision and protection. They believed that Asifa, in following Jesus, was effectively revoking her commitment to the family. Such "disloyalty" shamed her family, so they disowned her as a daughter and stopped providing for her.

In her family's mind, people abandon reciprocal relationships, like family, only for a new source of financial provision. So they keep asking, "How much did they pay you?" The family assumed that Asifa "sold her religion" (the Central Asian term for "conversion"). Though many things factored in Asifa's decision, her family understood their daughter's conversion through the lens of patronage. For good and bad, the dynamics of patronage inform the meaning of conversion in collectivistic, honor-shame contexts.

## THE ATONEMENT

Divine patronage is now available because Jesus atoned for sin. How did Jesus' death atone for the sin of ungrateful clients who dishonor the divine patron? How might patronage explain the saving significance of the cross? Anselm, a Benedictine monk and archbishop of Canterbury (c. 1033–1109), addressed this very issue in his book *Cur Deus Homo*. Anselm originally explained the incarnation and atonement of Jesus Christ through the medieval concept of lord-vassal patronage.[41]

> The social history of Anselm was characterized by feudalism, with the landowner, or "lord," living in peace with his vassals (or serfs) at the intersection of a carefully managed series of reciprocal obligations. The lord provided capital and protection; the serf provided honor, loyalty, and tribute. The stability of this social world rested on slavish fidelity and allegiance. In this context, Anselm's understanding of the atonement reads as a kind of allegory, with the lord as the Lord and the serfs as the human family. "Satisfaction" for us, in our criminal-justice system, has to do with the apprehension and punishment of

---

[41]This section on the atonement adapts my "Atonement for Honor-Shame Cultures," honorshame.com, April 10, 2017, http://honorshame.com/atonement-honor-shame-cultures-2/.

the guilty, while for Anselm and his contemporaries, satisfaction hinged on the fulfillment of certain obligations related to loyalty and honor.[42]

According to Anselm, humans are obligated to honor God by submitting to his will. Our disobedience dishonors God. In Anselm's words, "Whoever does not pay to God this honor due Him dishonors Him and removes from Him what belongs to Him; and this removal, or this dishonoring, constitutes a sin" (*CDH* I:11).[43] Because humans do not give to God the honor due his name, they incur an honor debt. "Everyone who sins is obliged to repay to God the honor which he has stolen" (*CDH* I:11). The honor which man owes God must be satisfactorily repaid because "God keeps nothing more justly than the honor of His dignity" (*CDH* I:13). God's justice rightly demands honor. Divine forgiveness requires the repayment of stolen honor (*CDH* I:12).

But regrettably, man is incapable of repaying his own honor debt to the divine lord. For the good deeds and worship we give to God are what we always owe him. So we "have nothing with which to make payment [of honor] for my sin" (*CDH* I:20). For this reason, the coming of the God-man was necessary for man's salvation (*CDH* II:4). Being sinless, Jesus was never indebted to God the Father, so he freely "gave Himself over to death for the honor of God" (*CDH* II:18). He thereby paid on behalf of sinners the honor debt which they owe to God. The gift of Jesus' life "satisfied" the honor debt incurred by our sins so that we do not experience God's honor-saving wrath.[44]

Because Jesus freely offered the great gift of his own life to God, the Father is obligated to reciprocate. "It is necessary for the Father to reward the Son. Otherwise, the Father would seem to be either unjust . . . or powerless" (*CDH* II:19). But since the Son needs nothing, God gives the reward

---

[42]Mark D. Baker and Joel B. Green, *Recovering the Scandal of the Cross: Atonement in New Testament and Contemporary Contexts*, 2nd ed. (Downers Grove, IL: IVP Academic, 2011), 22.

[43]All quotes are from Anselm, *Cur Deus Homo*, trans. Jasper Hoskins and Herbert Richardson (Minneapolis: The Arthur J. Banning Press, 2000), jasper-hopkins.info/CurDeusI.pdf and jasper-hopkins.info/CurDeusII.pdf, accessed Oct 15, 2016.

[44]When the honor debt is not satisfied, then God does punish. But punishment is not itself the repayment or "satisfaction." Anselm says, "*either* satisfaction *or* punishment must follow upon every sin" (CDH I:15, emphasis added). For Anselm the cross is not God's punishment, but a gift that satisfies our debt so that we are not punished.

of Jesus' gift to his human relatives in the form of forgiveness of sin. Jesus' sacrificial life generates an excess of infinite honor that overflows into our accounts.

Anselm also sees the death of Christ as an example "in order that no single human being would hesitate (when reason demands it) to render to God on behalf of himself that which one day he will summarily lose" (*CDH* II:18; cf. II:19). Jesus' life propels us to live as worthy clients who magnify our divine patron with sacrificial obedience.

At one point, Anselm discusses whether the necessity of God to save people actually "diminishes or eliminates gratitude to a benefactor" (*CDH* II:5). That is, if God saves us because he is honor-bound to preserve his own reputation, does that mean his favors do not deserve our thanks? Anselm responds with this distinction: when a person "confers a benefit against his will, little or no gratitude is owed to him. But when he willingly submits himself to the necessity of doing a good work . . . surely he deserves greater gratitude for his good work" (*CDH* II:5). So because God *willingly* accomplishes the good work he began with Adam, "we ought to attribute the entire good work to grace" (*CDH* II:5) and thereby give thanks to our divine benefactor.

Anselm's *Cur Deus Homo* provides a helpful starting point for contextualizing the atonement in terms of patronage, yet it could be more biblical in key ways. For one, "the heavenly Father in Anselm's essay plays a rather passive role of simply receiving honor through the cross," as though Jesus saves people *from* God.[45] But in fact, Jesus saves *as* God. The triune God, as the patron of the world, actively pursues and procures the restoration of all things for the glory of his grace.

We can affirm Anselm's basic concepts—God deserves honor; our sin dishonors God; his honor must be restored—but we should clarify *how* Jesus' death gives honor to God. For Anselm, God is righteous because he demands honor, like an absentee noble. However, in the Bible, God demonstrates his justice (i.e., the requirement that he be honored) by actively

---

[45]John Christopher Thomas and Frank D. Macchia, *Revelation*, THNTC (Grand Rapids: Eerdmans, 2016), 571.

saving.[46] Jesus brings honor to God because his death fulfills God's promise of universal blessing and enacts a new covenant (Romans 3:3-7; 15:8-9; Galatians 3:8, 14). For Anselm, God is righteous because he *demands* honor as a prerequisite for saving people. But in the Bible, God is righteous because he *displays* his honor by saving the nations.[47] God is righteous because he is a loyal patron who remains faithful, even to unworthy clients. The beneficent act of Jesus Christ is "God's fulfillment of longstanding promises made to Israel, presenting God as a reliable benefactor who has 'kept faith' with his historic body of clients (Lk 1:54, 68-75; Acts 3:26; Rom 15:8)."[48] In short, Anselm could have better interpreted the cross in light of God's suzerain-vassal covenant with Israel. Then his "satisfaction" theory of the atonement would be more in line with biblical theology. Nevertheless, Anselm's theology remains a helpful explanation of the cross in terms of patron-client relationships.

## CONCLUSION: THE GOSPEL ACCORDING TO PATRONAGE

The previous three chapters explain the theological categories of God, sin, and salvation through the paradigm of patronage. To pull these ideas together, we conclude this section with a gospel summary of salvation-history.[49]

> In the beginning, God created all things to display his power and glory. He is a patron-king whose benevolence and glory graces the entire earth. God provides and protects the entire human family, and he expects their loyal obedience.
>
> But the serpent tempted Adam and Eve to rebel against their patron. Satan promised they could become independent rulers instead of dependent clients. Humans disobeyed God, severing the patronage relationship. They dishonored the king and so faced the wrath of a slighted benefactor. The rebellion left the

---

[46]Mark A. Seifrid, *Christ, Our Righteousness: Paul's Theology of Justification* (Downers Grove, IL: IVP Academic, 2001), 44.

[47]These two options are not either-or dichotomies but more a matter of emphasis. For more, see Jackson Wu, *Saving God's Face: A Chinese Contextualization of Salvation through Honor and Shame*, Evangelical Missiological Society Dissertation Series (Pasadena, CA: William Carey Library, 2012), 193-292.

[48]deSilva, *Honor, Patronage, Kinship & Purity*, 128.

[49]Special thanks to Joy P. and Richard Yakoub, whose input and feedback enhanced this gospel summary.

human family dis-graced, living without God's benevolence and under Satan's bondage.

Then God initiates a new relationship with Abraham's family to mediate his glorious benefactions to the world. During the Exodus, God forms a special patronage relationship with Israel. According to the covenant, God would provide and protect Israel, and they should be loyal and obedient. God stays faithful to his special people, but Israel seeks patronage from human kings and false idols. They break covenant and dishonor God. Like Adam, Israel is dis-graced into exile. However, Israel's unfaithfulness does not nullify God's faithfulness. As a loyal patron, God keeps his promises of salvation.

The gift of God's own Son is the greatest act of divine beneficence. Jesus leaves his glorious throne to lavish God's favors upon disloyal rebels. He gives many benefactions—great feasts, liberation from dark forces, release from sins, protection from danger. In Jesus, the honorable patron is the perfect client. Jesus' complete obedience glorifies the Father. He repays the honor debt of Adam, Israel, and all humanity. This satisfies the just requirement for divine honor and remakes the covenant relationship. Jesus' death fulfills all of God's promises. In Jesus, God is a faithful and true patron to his people. Jesus rises from death and becomes the Supreme Broker of divine benefits. On our behalf, Jesus intercedes *to* the Father and mediates divine favors *from* the Father.

People who pledge their allegiance to Jesus' new kingdom receive God's benefactions—spiritual power, liberation from bondage, and release from sin. The beneficiaries of God's gift are not deserving clients; they are ungrateful sinners and rebellious enemies. To become God's favored clients, people must renounce false patrons and be loyal to Jesus. God gifts us his very Spirit, which transforms us into loyal clients who, rightly and finally, do honor God. God's new client-community embodies and mediates his radical generosity to the world. In the final day, God will gift complete life to those who glorify him and avenge all insults to his honor.

# PART FOUR

# MISSIONAL
# APPLICATIONS

# 10

# ENGAGING PATRONAGE

IMAGINE YOU SERVE IN CHINA, and a new couple has joined your ministry team. After one year of language learning, they approach you, saying, "I'm not sure about the Chinese language—all the corruption in this country is done in Chinese and the atheist government uses Chinese to control Christians. Because so much sin happens in the language, we have decided to stop speaking Chinese. Instead, we are just going to speak English at people, regardless of whether or not they understand us." Such a decision would be comical! Language is merely a tool for transferring meaning. The problem is not the language, but how sinful people misuse language. Likewise, the system of patronage is a social tool that can be used positively or negatively.

Recall how patronage functions as the grammar of relationships, the unstated rules that guide social interactions. If this is the case, rejecting patronage means rejecting relationships. For this reason, Christians must develop a biblical perspective on patronage. When patronage is the de facto system of social organization, Christians should ask: How can we function as biblical patrons? How can our patronage (and clientage) be God-centered and life-giving? These practical questions guide the next three chapters.

Relationships in patronage cultures involve navigating the tension between social realities and biblical ideals. On one hand, we cannot deny patronage as an ingrained relational concept, yet it often falls short of biblical ideals for relationships. So how might we engage imperfect patronage dynamics without forsaking biblical ideals? The framework of patronage is a "good enough" starting point for explaining Christian salvation or framing our relationships. Even societies with notoriously corrupt patronage have some concept of the "ideal benefactor"—someone who helps and gives out of genuine concern. So patronage has enough potential to be a starting point for relationship, but with time, must be transformed to reflect the biblical ideals of God-centered and life-giving patronage.

To navigate these waters, we first note the three main approaches to cultural patronage: rejection, adoption, or transformation.[1] These categories help mission practitioners understand the spectrum of possibilities for navigating patronage.

*Rejecting* patronage means remaining oblivious to the cultural system. This ethnocentric approach defaults to Western cultural practices (like the imaginary language learners in China). Rejecting patronage is rather common among Western missionaries who assume that egalitarian and bureaucratic forms of exchange are morally superior. This wholesale rejection of patronage is not a viable option.

*Adopting* patronage means functioning within the system for kingdom purposes. This approach appropriates the positive aspects of patronage to facilitate communication, make peace, foster relationships, bless people, and share the gospel.

*Transforming* patronage means redeeming the sinful elements of the system. This approach redeems the deficient aspects of patronage to engage people redemptively with kingdom values. Maturity is not outgrowing patronage but becoming a godly patron.

The biblical approach to patronage advocated in this book is straightforward—adopt the good and transform the bad. But in real life, distinguishing between good patronage and bad patronage is not always simple. For this reason, the next two chapters illustrate biblical patronage through a variety of practical examples.

## THE GOODNESS OF PATRONAGE

Tim was an American missionary who operated a business development center in Central Asia. After a staff Christmas celebration at the business center, everybody began cleaning up the dining room and washing up. Tim

---

[1]This paragraph is adapted from Jayson Georges and Mark D. Baker, *Ministering in Honor-Shame Cultures: Biblical Foundations and Practical Essentials* (Downers Grove, IL: IVP Academic, 2016), 141-43.

wanted to help out, so he grabbed the sponge and started scrubbing dishes. When Emal (the cook employed at the business center) saw her boss Tim working in the kitchen, she gasped in horror and demanded he stop. Her intense shock surprised Tim. So he put down the sponge and stepped aside.

Tim had intended to communicate appreciation by helping with the dishes, but Emal viewed his actions quite differently. For the boss/patron to do her job suggested she had failed at work; Emal felt embarrassed that her boss had to do her job. In hindsight, Tim realizes he could have expressed honor and appreciation to Emal through the honor-shame dynamic of patronage. For example, thanking her publicly or paying for her taxi ride home may have been better received. Patronage means using the role of respected leader who blesses and benefits other people. There are certainly instances when humility and service should override cultural expectations (see chapter eleven), but realize that your actions will be interpreted through the prism of patronage. Ignoring this fact may cause others to view you as a shameful (and shaming) person, regardless of your noble intentions.

Patronage can be challenging, frustrating, and even outright corrupt. Even Jesus himself could not avoid the challenges of patronage (Luke 22:24-27; John 13:5-8). But patronage is not inherently bad, and even has positive dimensions worth adopting in our relationships and ministry. We can follow the examples of Yahweh, Jesus, and Paul to make our relationships more God-centered and life-giving. Patronage is not a system of dependence, but a model of relational *inter*dependence. Functioning as a patron (or client) is an acceptable way to honor and love people. Through patronage, people of unequal status can relate loyally to one another with solidarity, generosity, and relational honor. Patronage motivated by sacrificial love for others is positive.[2]

Christians can leverage patronage to bless other people and accomplish God's missional purposes. A biblical patron stewards God's resources to bless people for God's glory. Missiologist Paul DeNeui says that leaders "who are most influential not only use their economic means to advance

---

[2]David Briones, "Paul's Intentional 'Thankless Thanks' in Philippians 4.10-20," *JSNT* 34, no. 1 (September 2011): 62 n. 63.

their patron status but have also gained the trust and respect of those whom they seek to save."[3] Christians can redeem elements of patronage for kingdom purposes. This chapter examines the upside of patronage in three areas of ministry: forming new relationships, enhancing existing relationships, and establishing ministry partnerships. The following points are not foolproof techniques but general advice for establishing meaningful relationships in patronage cultures.

## FORMING RELATIONSHIPS

Patronage can be helpful in forming genuine, reciprocal relationships. Del Chinchen, a veteran missionary in Africa, explains the social protocol for clients seeking potential benefaction, "It takes four steps to establish a relationship with a potential patron: admiration, visits, token gifts, and request."[4] To prepare the way for a positive response from the patron, clients first pay their respects to a patron by visiting and offering token gifts. This allows time for both sides to properly vet each other. After a period of "relational courtship," the potential client asks for material help. A contribution from the patron formalizes a long-term patron-client relationship.[5] This process is the patron-client dance. So if someone offers a gift or pays frequent visits, we can expect a relational opportunity (i.e., patronage) to follow. Unfortunately, many Westerners (such as me) miss these signals and respond negatively.

Danyar was a young Christian whom I thought I was discipling. We would meet weekly over tea to read the Bible and pray together. Danyar willingly read the Bible, but his financial requests gave me the impression he was more interested in material things than spiritual things. After several weeks of our meeting together, Danyar asked for a significant amount of money to pay his college tuition. Feeling uncomfortable mixing money with discipleship, I declined the request and suggested he

---

[3]Paul DeNeui, "Speaking of the Unspeakable: Money and Missions in Patron-Client Buddhist Cultures," in *Complexities of Money and Mission in Asia*, ed. Paul DeNeui (Pasadena, CA: William Carey Library, 2012), 116.

[4]Delbert Chinchen, "The Patron-Client System: A Model of Indigenous Discipleship," *EMQ* 31, no. 4 (October 1995), missionexus.org/the-patron-client-system-a-model-of-indigenous-discipleship/.

[5]Chechen, "The Patron-Client System."

ask his family for the money. After that conversation he stopped appearing for our weekly discipleship meetings. This confirmed my suspicions about his motive. I thought, "He really was only interested in my money." In hindsight I realize my actions likely surprised Danyar. He probably walked away wondering, "I thought we agreed to be friends. Why is Jayson reneging on our relationship now? If he purposefully declined to help me like that, I guess he does not want to be in a relationship with me anymore." My obliviousness to patron-client dynamics severed affected my relationship with Danyar.[6]

Chad was an American missionary who served in Haiti. The material poverty and foreign aid in Haiti creates many challenges in relationships between expatriates and national Haitians. Although Chad's ministry prioritized long-term solutions like job creation, he daily received requests for financial help. Like many people, Chad struggled to know, "When should I help?" As we talked, I proposed that Chad reframe the issue by asking, "When do I form a patronage relationship with someone?" This question helped Chad better assess the relational dynamics at play. Discerning when (and how) to help financially is complex, but the principles of biblical patronage can inform the process. When considering a patronage relationship, we should consider these three issues.

- *Will we see each other again?* A stranger at the door only expects a one-time handout. Seeing the person regularly is a basic prerequisite for a long-term relationship like patronage.

- *Will the relationship allow us to impart non-material resources?* In healthy relationships between a patron and client, the client receives spiritual instruction, friendship, and guidance. If the client seeks only material benefits, the relationship is distorted.

- *Will the recipient give something in return?* The relationship must be reciprocal; the client must be willing to offer something. This affirms the innate assets of all people. Mutuality is not about recipients' ability to repay financially in kind (Luke 6:33-35; 14:12-13), but their desire to contribute meaningfully to the relationship.

---

[6]Georges and Baker, *Ministering in Honor-Shame Cultures*, 152-53.

When giving and helping, what is best often depends on the relational and cultural context. Giving too much, or too little, can be harmful. But appropriate help depends on the situation. For example, some recipients feel burdened by a tremendous sense of debt and obligation. Wise patrons know how to give appropriately. For this reason, healthy patron-client relationships develop slowly, like a choreographed dance. This provides time, trust, and context to discern what level of exchange is actually life-giving.

Once you do form a patron-client relationship, you may expect it to be both (1) multidimensional and (2) long-lasting. Patronage involves fulfilling multiple social roles. Being a patron is not just handing out gifts like Santa Claus. Patrons are expected to do many things: adjudicate community problems, lead conversations, initiate relationships, and host large events. A patron is not a mere sugar daddy, but a respected person in the community who acts accordingly. Boaz in the Old Testament was a righteous wealthy person who took responsibility for others as a God-honoring, life-giving patron. Consider the many benefactions Boaz extended to Ruth and Naomi: he offers protection, food, and drink to the widows (Ruth 2:8-9), invites Ruth to the communal table (Ruth 2:14), pronounces a blessing for loyal actions (Ruth 3:10-11), assumes responsibility to resolving a social problem (Ruth 3:12-13), gifts an abundance of food (Ruth 3:15-17), convenes a village meeting (Ruth 4:1-3), restores ancestral land back to the family (Ruth 4:9), and bears a child to continue the lineage of his relative (Ruth 4:10-15). Boaz serves as a redeeming patron in multiple ways. His example shows how patronage is multidimensional.

Patronage is also an enduring commitment. The relationship does not end when you leave the country or a client finds a job. Westerners can quickly forget relational obligations, but the bonds of patronage are not easily unfettered. Patronage is a durable bond. The mutual devotion "can last a lifetime or be carried on from generation to generation by the descendants."[7] Two stories about King David (one positive and one negative) illustrate the longevity of patronage. When David establishes

---

[7]Delbert Chinchen, "The Return of the Fourth 'R' to Education: Relationships," *Missiology: An International Review* 25, no. 3 (July 1997): 332.

his kingdom, his first order of business is to show kindness upon the son of his deceased friend Jonathan. David says to Mephibosheth, "I will show you kindness for the sake of your father Jonathan; I will restore to you all the land of your grandfather Saul, and you yourself shall eat at my table always" (2 Samuel 9:7). King David cultivates a patronage relationship with Mephibosheth because of a prior relationship with his father Jonathan.

In a later story David forgets his clients and gets chastised. David has returned from exile and regains the throne in Jerusalem. Instead of celebrating the victory with sacrifices and feasts, David mourns the loss of his rebellious son Absalom (2 Samuel 19:1-4). His commander Joab explains to David, "Today you have covered with shame the faces of all your officers who have saved your life today, and the lives of your sons and your daughters, and the lives of your wives and your concubines, for love of those who hate you and for hatred of those who love you" (2 Samuel 19:5-6). David's public mourning inappropriately honored his rebellious son (i.e. "love of those who hate you") and broke covenant with his loyal soldiers and servants (i.e., "hatred of those who love you"). David forgot about his obligations as the patron to his officers. Once he realizes this relational error, David resumes his seat in Jerusalem and acknowledges his faithful soldiers with thanks. A patron-client relationship is an enduring bond. Patrons (and clients) should acknowledge this commitment when forming such relationships.

## An African View of Patronage

Paul is a 36-year old Cameroonian Christian. I met him as a translator during my visit in Yaoundé, Cameroon. After a few conversations with Paul, I realized he had the unique ability to explain his own culture with clear insight. Following is a transcription of an interview with him about patronage in May 2016. He provides an inside perspective on the tensions and nuances of patronage.

**What does the word "patron" mean in Cameroon?**

In Cameroon the French word *patron* is the word for "employer," the person who offers a job. The word also describes a wealthy person. Employees expect some favors from the *patron*, if he does his job well or goes an extra mile in certain things for the patron. For example, he could wash the car of the *patron*, even if it is not part of his job duty.

**What happens if the patron does not give favors to this employee or helper?**

If the employee did those things with the intention of catching the eye of the patron in one way or another, he feels frustrated when the patron is wicked or selfish. Most of the time it is intended to have financial favors, so if that does not come back to him he will think the patron is a wicked man. In French they would call him a "heartless" person; I hear this word the most. *Sheesh* means selfish or ungenerous and is also used for such people. But if the person suggests the patron is being "heartless" or *sheesh*, the patron will immediately mention whatever things they have provided, to look like a generous person.

**If a patron does give favors, what is the expectation from that person?**

Thank you is expected of course, but there is no expectation of singing the patron's praise to others. But, if the recipient says a negative word after receiving the benevolence, the patron will be very angry. Even if the person did significant things for the patron, the patron will forget what was done because of those words.

**What is a common mistake that Western missionaries make about patronage?**

Westerners are too careful trying not to hurt people, but because of that overprudence they end up hurting people. For example, if I visit a Western missionary and see their dirty car, I think it is absurd such a person would drive a dirty car. If it was my father's car, I would have to fetch water to wash it. But in this case, there is a hose nearby. So I wash the car out of joy! It is easy to do it! But, if they feel, "Oh, my employee washed my car, I need to pay him." If they do that all the time, I feel offended. They think I just want money all the time; that gets offensive. It is not bad if once in a while they give me a tip. But if I do it many times and they do not give me a tip, I'm like, "They are so *sheesh*!" The idea is for Westerners to believe that Africans believe more in relationships. That is a high value for them—relationships. I do not expect to be paid, but I expect appreciation. That means for them to realize I did something and say, "thank you."

## ENHANCING RELATIONSHIPS

The nuances of patronage can strengthen relationships in a variety of ways. This section applies patronage to work relationships, teaching relationships, and peacemaking to illustrate a few ways Christians can leverage patronage.

**Work relationships.** In the West, an employer's responsibility generally ends with the paycheck. Work relationships are limited to the workplace. But in the Majority World, employing someone creates an implicit patron-client relationship. The boss assumes broad responsibility for employees. They might pay medical bills, offer marriage advice, and cover last-minute tuition fees for the employee. Bosses are expected to help resolve non-work problems. On the flipside, employers expect an employee's loyalty to extend beyond their official job description. The relationship is multidimensional (which can feel like "endless expectations"!). In this context of patronage, an employer's involvement beyond the office forms a more intimate bond that expresses genuine care and concern. Of course, not all employers function as a benevolent patron in this way, but the system of patronage does make this ideal a possibility we can strive towards.

Social and business entrepreneurs also function as clients who acknowledge their key patrons. In high-networked societies, the success of a ministry or work project depends upon the goodwill of gatekeepers. Our team in Central Asia worked among villages in the countryside. We provided various benefits in the rural communities, such as conducting English classes, distributing Samaritan's Purse boxes, and purchasing local commodities for export. As Westerners entering in a conservative Muslim village, we leveraged patronage to overcome barriers. We asked the community leader(s) to facilitate public gatherings and sought public opportunities to acknowledge their indispensable role. This portrayed the local leader as the honorable patron who was protecting and providing for his people. This fostered goodwill and enhanced access to the community.

**Teaching relationships.** The dynamics of patronage greatly influence teacher-student relationships. This reality affects people teaching in any context—i.e., an English club, a Bible school, or a medical clinic. Western education emphasizes individual achievement, limits the teacher-student relationship to the classroom, and tightly follows accreditation regulations. Educational institutions in the Majority World contexts operate differently. They may have extensive policies, but in practice "the actual processes are based on patronage and exemption."[8]

Students in a collectivistic culture sense that "it is impossible to succeed in life independently. These students find it necessary to link up with the teacher through a personal relationship in order to succeed in the classroom."[9] The student expects patron-teachers to provide knowledge, guidance, and essential resources for success in life. So students focus on cultivating a tight relationship. Students often assume, "The more respect shown to the teacher, the more knowledge one receives."[10] Gestures of respect include: carrying the teacher's bag, standing upon the teacher's entrance, always agreeing with the teacher, offering token gifts of appreciation, and praising the quality of instruction. Western teachers who reject the patronage system and refuse to receive respect from client-students undermine the educational process and relationship. Del Chinchen explains the adverse consequences:

> The teacher blocks the student's goal of involving the teacher in his or her learning endeavor. The teacher not only rejects this precious collective value of society, but also, unwittingly, rejects the student. The negative attitude towards this teacher ripples across the entire student body. . . . This type of teacher makes it impossible for the student to reciprocate. As mentioned earlier, without reciprocity there is no relationship. The student becomes buried in the debt of knowledge gained which he or she cannot possibly repay, leading to his or her own social negation.[11]

But a teacher who relates to students as a parental, caring patron establishes personal relationships of genuine reciprocity and empowers students to receive knowledge. An effective teacher fulfills the students' desires for a life mentor who guides them through academic studies and equips them to succeed beyond the classroom.

---

[8]Perry Shaw, "Patronage, Exemption, and Institutional Policy," *EMQ* 49, no. 1 (January 2013): 8.
[9]Chinchen, "The Return of the Fourth 'R'," 321.
[10]Chinchen, "The Return of the Fourth 'R'," 328.
[11]Chinchen, "The Return of the Fourth 'R'," 328-29.

***Peacemaking.*** Patronage can help resolve conflict. In many cultures, becoming a client is a strategic way to make peace. This, in effect, means finding a patron to help resolve the issue. By requesting help from a patron, potential clients deliberately put themselves under another person to get help and save face. Becoming a client utilizes the social network and capital of that person to address a dilemma. In *Cross-Cultural Conflict* Duane Elmer explains how this works.

> Generally, if one holds the power to keep another person from being shamed, that person is morally obligated to do something to keep shame from coming to the other. However if the person does not act to save another's honor, she or he is in danger of losing face and being shamed.[12]

Depending on the culture, the art of making a patronage connection may involve presenting a token gift with the request or directly saying, "I have this (embarrassing) problem. Can you help me?" This invites people to assume the responsibility of patron and help solve the problems. People generally relish the opportunity to help because this enhances their name. People feel honored when others request help because it implies they possess the social clout to fix problems. It may seem counterintuitive for a "rich Westerner" to become a client in a "developing country." But as an outsider living in their country, remember that you are the guest in this situation who receives from the host country.

The following story about Trevor and Norma, Canadian missionaries in the Philippines, shows how they leveraged patronage in a ministry relationship. They learned to repay the "debt of gratitude," and doors opened. They recount:

> For 24 years, our main tribal ministry in the Philippines was mostly funded by one wealthy Chinese businessman. This man, Mr. Wu, used to treat us to elaborate feasts at expensive restaurants. Whenever we tried to take him out for a meal, he still managed to foot the bill. We invited him to see our ministry first-hand and to host him lavishly, but he declined, claiming he was nervous about rebel hostage-taking during the ride from Manila to the "wilds" of the

---

[12]Duane Elmer, *Cross-Cultural Conflict: Building Relationships for Effective Ministry* (Downers Grove, IL: IVP Academic, 1993), 80-81. Elmer's entire chapter "The One-Down Position and Vulnerability" examines this channel for conflict resolution.

countryside. Because he gave tens of thousands of pesos every year, we never felt like we could fully repay him for his generosity. We tried to give him gifts like a soapstone sculpture from Canada to show our appreciation, but Mr. Wu told us not to bother with gifts. His office is cluttered with gifts from various clients. He would say in his broken English, "Just thanks God." So we complied and stopped trying to repay him, except through our prayers.

Mr. Wu and his extended family started out as our "clients" many years ago because Trevor's parents had discipled Mr. Wu's family when he was just a teenager. By the time Trevor grew up and returned to the Philippines as a missionary himself, Mr. Wu and all his siblings had become successful and wealthy. But they felt *utang na loob* ("debt of gratitude") to my husband's clan. We were his patrons because of the spiritual impact that Trevor's parents had on his family. In the Philippines context, *utang na loob* is tied very closely to the patron-client relationship. The client has an *utang na loob* to repay to his patron. To repay his *utang na loob*, Mr. Wu led the funding of our ministry. Over time the roles reversed. Because of his wealth and continuous financial support, he became our patron and we were his clients. We went every year to report on our ministry. We always felt like we were groveling, but Mr. Wu assured us God was prompting his giving. In fact, over the years he gave vehicles and a motorcycle. But as Westerners not in tune with shame-honor or patron-client roles, we did not notice the shift in roles. We kept accepting his gifts, not realizing that we had become clients and now we had an *utang na loob* to Mr. Wu.

After several years, Mr. Wu began showing signs of donor fatigue. His giving became sporadic and he became harder to contact. His secretary started screening our calls and blocking our attempts to talk or meet with him. Mr. Wu then suggested a phase-out contract, drawn up by a lawyer, where his giving would decline gradually, leaving our ministry to fund itself after about 5 years. Perhaps in his mind, he had fully repaid his *utang na loob* to my husband's family. We considered options of closing the ministry or reformatting it to survive with no funds.

Our relationship gradually deteriorated with Mr. Wu's secretary. We racked our brains trying to figure out what we could do to re-establish the relationship. When visiting Cambodia to attend a ministry seminar about honor and shame, we learned about patronage. So, we thought of buying a Cambodian silk scarf for his secretary for Christmas. Then we realized that we should do the same for all the ladies in Mr. Wu's family, all of whom had contributed to the funds that Mr. Wu had given to us. Then later we got the idea of baking Christmas cookies as gifts. We baked and organized cookies on plates and wrapped them for four days.

The results were amazing! When my husband delivered the Christmas cookies and scarves the Saturday before Christmas—in the pouring rain of a typhoon—only Mr. Wu's secretary was in the office. Her usual cold reception absolutely melted when she saw the gifts. She became all smiles and sweetness, and promised to make sure all the packages were delivered. Trevor even told her that since she was the first one to see the scarves, she could have first pick of any color she wanted—even before Mr. Wu's family. The following Monday, Mr. Wu, who had been unreachable for several years and who had not given any money in over a year (a breach of his own contract), phoned us several times to asked how he could immediately transfer funds to the ministry's bank account. Within days he and his family had given more money than he had contracted and funded the work through the entire year! Then, one member of his family gave a substantial money gift to each of our children. No mention was ever made of the cookies or scarves. We, the client, had repaid our *utang na loob*, and the relationship was restored. There was no need for verbal thanks, but only for action demonstrating appreciation.

Spending four hectic days before Christmas baking cookies was hard. But for as long as God gives us this patron-client relationship, I will block off the week before Christmas to bake and we will make a special trip for our Christmas deliveries. How could I do otherwise after such a vivid illustration of the power of the patron-client relationship in the Asian context?[13]

The ethics of patronage can be complex. Are the "financial friendships" of patronage morally acceptable? Is it right to give gifts to gain special access? Should Christians go along with social inequality? Human sin can turn systems of patronage into corruption. During my initial years in Central Asia, patronage angered me. But as I reflected on my experiences, I realized my initial objections to the structures of patronage came from my own pride and ethnocentrism—I assumed my cultural system for exchanging good and services was superior, and their system of patronage must be replaced with Western alternatives. Over time I realized patronage

---

[13]Originally published as "The Patron-Client Relationship in a Philippine Context," in *eLINK Newsletter* (2016). With the author's permission, this version has been slightly adapted for readability. Permission to publish granted by publisher and original author.

simply uses honor as a form of payment instead of cash. Can we use a different currency to buy something? Assuming justice is not perverted, I believe that we can. Having come to appreciate the nuances of patron-client systems, I now feel callous during economic exchanges in America—I give the cashier money and take the items without any sort of relationship. That may be legal, but not nearly as honoring. Rules and laws ensure equality and predictability, but they can minimize human interaction. In contrast, patron-client systems foster relationships and community. Whether we like it or not, we must know people to get things. Becoming a client means setting aside Western preferences and humbly depending upon other people for help.

## ESTABLISHING "PARTNERSHIPS"

An American missions agency had a fruitful ministry in Africa during the 1900s. Thousands of churches spread throughout multiple countries. Over the decades, the relationship matured as the African churches assumed responsibility. The relationship between the Western agency and African churches involved financial decisions and capital projects. So to avoid confusion and miscommunication, the American missions agency said all "partnerships" would be defined in clear agreements.

One day the African church leaders asked a missionary of the American agency, "When will the mission agency build a Bible Institute for our churches?" The American missionary reminded them, "The terms of our partnership have been clearly laid out. When the African church collects the first 20 percent to buy the land, then our agency will fund the remaining 80 percent to build the facilities. The African church must fulfill their end of the partnership, and the American side will complete our part of the relationship."[14]

Considering the history of the Western missions enterprise, this approach was an admirable leap forward. However, as I heard the American missionary say "partnership," I wondered, "What comes to the Africans' mind when they hear that word *partnership*?" For the American, the phrase

---

[14]I personally witnessed this conversation in May 2016. The quotes are not verbatim but summarize the longer conversation.

"complete our side of the relationship" means fulfill the terms of the written contract. But to the Africans, I suspect that the "complete our side of the relationship" involves expectations of patronage. Is "partnership" the most helpful (or even realistic) approach to crosscultural relationships? The history of money in Western missions illuminates this sensitive issue.

From the year 1800 into the early 1900s, paternalism was the primary approach of the Western missionary enterprise. Some forward-thinking missiologists advocated for self-governing and self-financing churches,[15] but nevertheless, missionaries on the ground often mirrored colonial powers and related to Majority World churches in controlling, paternalistic ways.

The mid-1900s brought winds of change. Many colonized countries gained their independence after World War II (1941–1945). Churches in the Global South sought religious independence from Western Christianity and called for a "moratorium on missions" from the West. This desire for independence was a natural corrective to the paternalism and dependence of the bygone colonial era.

During this same period, the church in the Global South experienced incredible growth. This explosion of Christianity in Asia, Africa, and Latin America required a new relational model, something between paternalism and independence, to structure the relationships between Western and Majority World churches. In the 1990s the term *partnership* began trending in missions literature.[16]

The term *partnership* has been a healthier middle ground between paternalism and independence (see figure 10.1). Partnerships form genuine relationships (unlike independence) and affirm mutual dignity (unlike paternalism). Even the U2 singer Bono recognizes, "Paternalism—the old way

[15]E.g., Rufus Anderson, Henry Venn, John Nevius, and Roland Allen.

[16]Luis Bush and Lori Lutz, *Partnering in Ministry: The Direction of World Evangelism* (Downers Grove, IL: InterVarsity Press, 1990); Phil Butler, *Partnership: Accelerating Evangelism in the 90s* (n.p.: Interdev, 1995); James Kraakevik and Dotsey Welliver, eds., *Partners in the Gospel: The Strategic Role of Partnership in World Evangelization* (Wheaton, IL: Billy Graham Center, 1992); John Maxwell and Tim Elmore, *The Power of Partnership in the Church* (Nashville: Thomas Nelson, 1999); Daniel Rickett, *Making Your Partnership Work* (Enumclaw, WA: Wine Press Publishing, 2002; Roswell, GA: Daniel Rickett, 2014); William Taylor, ed. *Kingdom Partnerships for Synergy in Missions* (Pasadena, CA: William Carey Library, 1994). For a concise historical overview of partnership in missions, see Enoch Wan and Kevin P. Penman, "The 'Why,' 'How' and 'Who' of Partnership in Christian Missions," *GM* 3, no. 7 (March 2010), ojs.globalmissiology.org/index.php/english/article/viewFile/61/179.

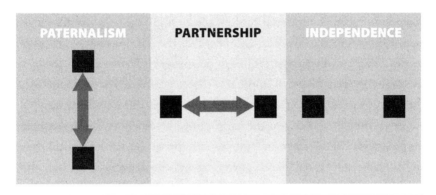

**Figure 10.1.** Models for international relationships

we did development—is no match for partnership."[17] Given the three options of paternalism, partnership, and independence, partnership is certainly
the healthiest model for crosscultural relationships.

However, the English word *partnership* assumes Western values like
egalitarianism and autonomy. But Majority World peoples value hierarchy
and reciprocity. So, we must ask: Does the model of Western conception
of *partnership* impose a foreign model on relationships? Might *patronage*
be a more appropriate, life-giving model for crosscultural relationships?

Social inequality is an indisputable fact of life in many cultures. The
Wolof people of Senegal have a proverb: "When two persons greet each
other, one has shame, the other has glory."[18] In nearly all relationships,
there are superiors and inferiors, haves and have-nots, patrons and clients.
This does not deny the inherent worth of all people and cultures but acknowledges the economic realities of our fallen world. Despite our good
intentions, merely using the word *partnership* does not erase economic
privilege and social hierarchy. The approach of biblical patronage affirms
mutuality and inherent dignity yet acknowledges the reality of economic
imbalances and social inequalities.

Requiring our relationships to be partnerships (in the Western sense of
the word) can impose outside assumptions onto the relationship. Some

---

[17]*Poverty, Inc.*, directed by Michael Matheson Miller (Warren, NJ: Passion River Films, 2016), 1:24:55.
[18]Quoted from David Maranz, *African Friends and Money Matters* (Dallas, TX: SIL International,
    2001), 128.

aspects of partnership—such as status equality—appear offensive and immoral in hierarchical cultures. Tim (an American) led a student ministry in Central Asia. The oldest and most capable national member of the team was Riskeldi. Tim sought to develop and empower Riskeldi to assume future leadership. Though Tim was older and organizationally higher than Riskeldi, he went out of his way to relate to him as an equal peer. Tim gave Riskeldi the freedom to initiate and execute his own ideas for the student ministry. He was purposefully not directive or authoritative. Tim assumed the relationship was fine, until it blew up. Tim then learned that Riskeldi had interpreted his "empowering partnership" as abandonment and neglect. Riskeldi desired for Tim, his elder and superior, to provide clear directives and oversight, but felt like Tim withheld resources and attention. Tim's intentions, though pure and noble, were misinterpreted. Through conversations Tim eventually learned patronage was a more appropriate relational model for communicating concern, respect, and empowerment to Riskeldi. Patronage would allow them to relate in a socially acceptable and mutually beneficial way, even as social unequals. Instead of assuming that a Western-style partnership is the only model for crosscultural ministry relationships, we should remain open to the Majority World model of patronage.

Proposing patronage as a biblical model for relationships does require several qualifications. First, we should not assume that the Westerner is the patron. Even for Westerners serving in developing countries, the relational model of clientage might be more suitable than partnership, as various stories throughout this book illustrate. Second, this discussion does not suggest that patronage is better or more biblical than partnership, but only that patronage can sometimes be a viable and more realistic model for relationships. The goal of crosscultural relationships should actually be stewardship—managing resources and relationships for kingdom purposes (Matthew 25:14-30). Both patronage and partnerships, I propose, can be appropriate models of biblical stewardship (see figure 10.2).

The aim of Christian relationships is love—the affirmation and demonstration of someone's inherent worth. In Western culture, such dignifying love is generally expressed through social equality. But in the Majority

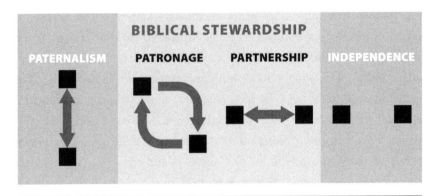

**Figure 10.2.** Biblical stewardship in international relationships

World, mutual relationships communicate love and worth. People base identity on social connections and being in community. In such contexts, patronage, even with an element of social inequality, may be the best way to affirm value and communicate love.

Of course, not all instances of patronage are acceptable. Patronage that is corrupt, abusive, and destructive is not biblical patronage. So, then, how can we transform power-grabbing, manipulative patronage into God-centered, life-giving patronage? This is the topic of the next chapter.

# 11

# TRANSFORMING RELATIONSHIPS

HEATHER CHO WAS THE VICE PRESIDENT AT KOREAN AIR. Her shocking behavior aboard a Korean Air flight in December 2014 became a viral news story. The *Washington Post* reported:

> Sitting in first class aboard a Korean Air due to fly to Seoul, Cho was handed some macadamia nuts by a flight attendant, though she had not asked for any. Worse still, the nuts were handed to her in a bag, and not on a plate, as per Korean Air rules. Cho was dismayed by the flouting of company guidelines. After reprimanding the flight attendant who handed her the nuts, she demanded that the plane, now on the taxiway, return to the gate and that chief flight attendant exit the plane. Witnesses told the Korea Times that she shouted during the incident. The flight, with 250 people aboard, was delayed by 11 minutes as a result.[1]

Koreans strongly condemned the "nut rage" tantrum as aristocratic arrogance and privilege particularly since her father was the Chairman of the airline. She resigned four days after the event, and Korean courts sentenced her to a year in prison. The reason her behavior angered fellow Koreans is worth noting. The outcry against Cho was not against her role as a patron, as a Westerner might assume, but her "inappropriate behavior as a *Gap* [i.e., patron leader] who should have been more benevolent."[2] The chief judge in her case stated, "If she were considerate to people, if she didn't treat

---

[1]Adam Taylor, "CEO's Daughter Loses Job after 'Nut Rage' Incident on Korean Air Flight," *Washington Post*, December 9, 2014, www.washingtonpost.com/news/worldviews/wp/2014/12/09/ceos-daughter -loses-job-after-nut-rage-incident-on-korean-air-flight/.

[2]Robert Oh, "Patron-Client Dynamics Between Korean Missionaries and Cambodian Christians," *Asia Missions Advance* 48 (July 2015): 17.

employees like slaves, if she could have controlled her emotion, this case would not have happened."[3] Cho acted like a malevolent patron who misused her power.

Patronage has many dark sides: angry demands; domineering leadership; manipulation; deceit; false hopes; bribery; status grasping; revenge; suppression and silencing; corruption; and so on. The system can devolve into outright exploitation. Bad patronage decimates relationships.

Even "gifts" can be poisonous when people manipulate social expectations to their advantage. Gifts from powerful patrons can enslave clients with an unpayable debt. The powerful extend help to suck followers into their webs of control.[4] On the other side, gifts from conniving clients manipulate influencers and pervert justice. Like the Trojan Horse, gifts can become a secret ruse to gain access and power over people.

A problem with patronage is the tendency of sinful people to dehumanize others for selfish gain. Patrons treat clients as slaves, and clients treat patrons as vending machines. Corrupted patrons enforce a rigid hierarchy; they require honorific titles and squelch dissent. They diminish others and elevate themselves to increase the social distance. Worldly patrons keep clients down to maintain their privileged position.

Clients capitulate by placing their unbridled hope and trust in patrons. Propelled by the basic need to survive, they relinquish personal agency and sell their voice to the highest-bidding patron. At its worst, the patron-client exchange becomes purely instrumental. When patronage gets corrupted, patrons become *more than* humans, and clients become *less than* humans.

## TRANSFORMING PATRONAGE

Just like abusive husbands do not invalidate the institution of marriage, the problems of patronage do not invalidate the entire social model. Rather, the sinful abuses call Christians to purposefully redeem the system. In the Bible, we see how people change patronage from the inside out.

---

[3]Youkyung Lee, "Korean Air Nut Rage Exec Sentenced to 1 Year in Prison," *USA Today*, February 12, 2015, www.usatoday.com/story/news/world/2015/02/12/korea-nut-rage-sentenced/23280231/.
[4]Larry S. Persons, *The Way Thais Lead: Face as Social Capital* (Chiang Mai, Thailand: Silkworm Books, 2016), 109.

God does not destroy human cultures but rather enters them and redeems them from within. God is present in the patron-client system. . . . A patron-client system can be God-honoring, as can be seen in the fact that most of the cultures of the Bible are patron-client in their orientation.[5]

The kingdom of God transforms sinful patronage into biblical patronage. The following chart (table 11.1) distinguishes corrupted patronage from transformed patronage.[6]

|  | CORRUPTED PATRONAGE | TRANSFORMED PATRONAGE |
| --- | --- | --- |
| **Gifts** | Bribery, coercive intent | Token symbols, express thanks |
| **Expectations** | False hopes, false securities | Honesty, integrity |
| **Bond** | Weak, instrumental | Strong, affective |
| **Relationship** | Utilitarian, materialistic | Genuine, moral |
| **Patron** | Insists on status, possessive | Nurtures others, life-giving |
| **Demeanor** | Paternalistic, superior | Collaborative, interdependent |

**Table 11.1.** Corrupted vs. transformed patronage

In corrupted patronage, God is absent and the patron-client relationship is notably hierarchical. Whereas biblical patronage understands patron-client exchanges as part of God's provision for people. God is the ultimate Patron. Human patrons simply mediate his gifts and direct the praise back to him. A biblical patron also works to minimize the social distance with clients. Biblical patronage resists the sinful tendency to oppress clients and exalt human patrons. Figure 11.1 visualizes these contrasting paradigms.

Christians pursue the social paradigm of *God-centered* and *life-giving* patronage in their relationships. This chapter discusses principles and examples for transforming patronage under three headings: minimizing social distance, glorifying God, and receiving life.

---

[5]Paul DeNeui, "Speaking of the Unspeakable: Money and Missions in Patron-Client Buddhist Cultures," in *Complexities of Money and Mission in Asia*, ed. Paul DeNeui (Pasadena, CA: William Carey Library, 2012), 127.

[6]Adapted from Delbert Chinchen, "The Patron-Client Relationship Concept: A Case Study from the African Bible Colleges in Liberia and Malawi," (unpublished PhD diss., Biola University, 1994), 179.

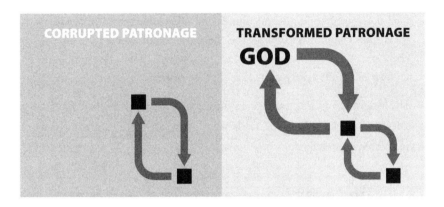

**Figure 11.1.** Corrupted and transformed patronage

## MINIMIZING SOCIAL DISTANCE

Transformed patronage works against the natural tendency to exalt patrons and minimize clients. Christians should intentionally limit the asymmetrical social gap. One effective way to rebalance patron-client relationships is to reverse the exchange process. Patrons should seek opportunities to give honor to the client. This posture allows the relationships to be fluid and dynamic, which enhances the reciprocity and depth of the relationship. In the following example, Mark Baker purposefully reverses the patron-client exchange. By seeking advice and giving thanks, he positions himself as a client.

> Antonio was a Honduran friend and partner in ministry. Through partici-
> pating in various workshops and experimentation on his own small farm
> he had become a gifted community development worker in the area of
> sustainable agriculture—something I knew next to nothing about. We lent
> and gave him money at various points. He clearly felt indebted to us in a
> patron-client way. I did not openly reject his comments or actions that
> treated me as patron. I did, however, intentionally seek ways to level the
> relationship by treating him as my gardening consultant. Every time he
> would visit I would take him to look at my compost pile and garden. I asked
> him for direction and advice. I always thanked him and underlined that
> any success in the garden was due to his guidance. When we visited him I
> would always ask for a tour of his farm and inquire about new methods.

I told him he was my teacher and sought to take the posture of student, as a different kind of patron.[7]

The apostle Paul developed a similar relationship with the Corinthians. He frames their relationship as mutual brokers of God's gifts. In 2 Corinthians 1:3-11, Paul and the Corinthians are co-clients in God's economy. Paul's ministry brings "consolation and salvation" to the Corinthians (2 Corinthians 1:3-7). He endures hardships as a tangible embodiment of Christ's own suffering on their behalf. Then in 2 Corinthians 1:8-10, the flow of God's graces shifts directions. Paul says his deliverance from future peril will come about as the Corinthians broker God's favor to the apostle himself (2 Corinthians 1:11). Paul relies on the Corinthians to channel God's graces, and he expects them to pray and access divine resources on his behalf. God grants comfort to both parties so they can forward those graces to fellow suffers. David Briones explains Paul's vision for such "mutual patronage"

> creates a community of alternating disequilibrium, having been "bound together by webs of need and of gift," which distributes divine commodity to those in need (cf. 2 Cor 8:13-15), eradicates self-sufficiency, and renders every inhabitant equally dependent on God through the agency of others; and that promotes a counter-cultural lifestyle that lives by the way of the cross rather than the way of this world, by the path of other-regarding shame rather than self-gratifying honour.[8]

Paul nurtures an interdependent relationship of mutual benefaction with the Corinthian community. This is a feature of God's eschatological salvation. In a world where most patrons require clients to "kiss their ring," patrons who look to receive from clients subvert the status quo. Such transformed patronage does not imply both parties become exact equals in status, for that would be confusing and shaming. However, the reciprocal exchange does become *more* balanced.

In many countries, to employ house help creates a patron-client relationship. In Central Asia, workers expect a meal during work hours but

---

[7]Jayson Georges and Mark D. Baker, *Ministering in Honor-Shame Cultures: Biblical Foundations and Practical Essentials* (Downers Grove, IL: IVP Academic, 2016), 150.

[8]David Briones, "Mutual Brokers of Grace: A Study in 2 Corinthians 1.3-11," *NTS* 56, no. 4 (Oct 2010): 553-54.

typically eat in a different location (the physical distance symbolizes social distance). One day I came home during lunchtime. My wife and daughter were eating at our dining table, but our new house helper Mukada was eating alone in the kitchen. My wife had invited her to sit at the table, but Mukada declined. Even after I invited her to join us, she looked down and declined (to show that she understood "her place"). I wanted to communicate to Mukada that "her place" was different, so I played the shame card in her favor. "I would be insulted," I said, "if you did not sit with us." My comment surprised her. I suggested our meal was not complete until she joined us; we wanted her at the table. By eating alone, she was robbing us of the honor of her presence. Mukada intuited that social logic and joined us at the table as a guest. Giving honor to someone in a client position is an important way to lessen the social distance.

Another key part of functioning as a patron is learning to accept various forms of repayment from clients. Instead of expecting people to repay financially, patrons must consider the assets clients can offer. Wealth is not just financial in nature. If we find ourselves relating to a client, we ask, "What could this person offer to others?" This question dignifies people by affirming the innate assets and resources that they *can* give. Many clients can offer personal connections, cultural knowledge, and their time. People in collectivistic societies possess a network of acquaintances. So for example, those traveling to a new town can ask one of their "borrowers" if they have a relative who lives in that town. Those who need a document from a government office can ask a client if they know someone who works there. Granting an outsider access to the client's social web expresses thanks and loyalty for the outsider's patronage. Also, asking cultural questions postures foreigners as learners receiving the gift of knowledge from the client. And when patrons have a problem, they consult with the person—"I'm facing this problem and need your advice." This mere comment implies the person has wisdom to offer. Finally, clients have (or will find) spare time to help. This may involve finding creative ways for people to repay the patron by completing manual tasks, but it nevertheless allows the client to contribute something to the relationship.

In transformed patronage each side serves the other and resources flow both ways. Reciprocity is essential to the ongoing relationship. Patrons who do not receive from clients bury them under mounds of social debt. Delbert Chinchen explains,

> The system [of patronage] requires that the patron be needy and empathetic. American missionaries tend to be self-sufficient. It's hard for them to be needy. But not to receive from others makes them look superior. If you have no needs, invent them. Ask clients to give valuable information in the community, to help with language study, and to advise on cultural issues. My wife and I had helped a student [David] by bringing his wife out of danger in Liberia so that she could deliver her baby in Côte d'Ivoire. When we returned to Liberia several months later, David reciprocated. He planted a large garden of sweet corn just for us, and brought the corn when he knew we needed it.[9]

These practical ideas for minimizing social distance foster life and flourishing. They create and sustain conditions for others to exercise authority and experience shalom. Such patrons understand that clients are not their own possession (cf. John 6:66-67) but people with agency and giftings that can benefit others. Benevolent patrons empower clients to give to others, perhaps in a way greater than themselves (cf. John 14:12). True power, as Andy Crouch describes, "is to make room for others to act with authority. We measure our lives increasingly by what others have done—and received credit for—thanks to our advocacy."[10] Life-giving patronage creates pathways for clients to become godly patrons who help others. In *The Way Thais Lead: Face as Social Capital*, Larry Parsons presents this compelling portrait of virtuous patron-leaders.

> [They] treat subordinates with respect and honor them appropriately. They train them to do good works for the sake of doing good, not for the sake of increased "face-eyes." . . . Virtuous leaders focus on the intrinsic worth of others, not on discrepancies in power. They exude a gracious demeanor that reduces the feeling of distance between them and others. They honor subordinates who are worthy of honor. They are pleased when good people ascend from the hierarchy below. They are not threatened by the process of worthy protégés, because they remember that, inevitably, their own time must pass.[11]

---

[9]Delbert Chinchen, "The Patron-Client System: A Model of Indigenous Discipleship," *EMQ* 31, no. 4 (October 1995), missionexus.org/the-patron-client-system-a-model-of-indigenous-discipleship/.

[10]Andy Crouch, *Strong and Weak* (Downers Grove, IL: IVP Books, 2016), 175.

[11]Persons, *Way Thais Lead*, 194-95.

## GLORIFY GOD

Worldly patrons use patronage to enhance their own status. For example, philanthropists get their names on big buildings or politicians dip their fingers into lucrative industries. But followers of Jesus transform the ultimate aim of patronage from human glory to divine glory. Sharing financial resources and meeting material needs brings glory to God. True benefaction stewards God's finances for God's purposes. Instead of receiving the praise and honor for themselves, Christian patrons direct loyalties to God so that his name gets honored. The gospel transforms patronage to make God all-in-all, the ultimate Patron who gives gifts and receives praises. In this way, patronage becomes an act of worship (Philippians 4:18).

The stories of King Herod and Paul in Acts juxtapose the two types of patronage: blasphemous patronage and God-exalting patronage.

In Acts 12:20-23, King Herod welcomes clients from Tyre and Sidon into his court, but not without putting his status on full display. He dresses in royal attire and sits on the elevated platform. From below, the people shout out praises worthy of the gods. Herod considers himself the ultimate giver who is worthy of such adoration. He steals the glory that belongs to God alone. Immediately he loses his status before everyone. God strikes him dead and worms consume his mortal body, a sign of abject disgrace. Herod abused his position as patron-king to receive worship for himself. This story is a sobering reminder to all earthly patrons—the pursuit of glory ends in shame (Proverbs 3:34; James 4:6; 1 Peter 5:5).

Then in Acts 14, we encounter a God-centered example of patronage. The apostle Paul heals a man crippled from birth (Acts 14:8). In antiquity, granting freedom from illness was a common benefit of patronage (as in Acts 4:9; 10:38). The Lycaonians who witnessed Paul's miraculous authority wanted to thank and worship him with a sacrifice. They perceive Paul to be divine, so respond as grateful clients.

The response of Paul and Barnabas is strong and immediate. First, they tear their clothes in public defiance of the Lycaonians' thinking. The apostles insist they are mere mortals and redirect the conversation to the Creator God, who is the ultimate provider and patron. God alone has made heaven and earth and seas and everything in them. This God has faithfully provided plentiful rains and harvests to all people. The implication of Paul's words is obvious—the Lycaonians' praise rightfully belongs to God, not to the messengers who bring his gifts (cf. Acts 3:10-16). The apostles' God-exalting patronage stands in stark contrast with Herod's blasphemous patronage (see table 11.2). Biblical patronage glorifies God as the original giver who deserves all praise.

| PATRONAGE CYCLE | HEROD (ACTS 12:20–23) | PAUL (ACTS 14:8–17) |
|---|---|---|
| 1. Patron's Benevolence | Herod addresses client nations from his throne. | Paul commands a lame man in Lystra to walk. |
| 2. Client's Gratitude | People shout, "The voice of a god, and not of a mortal!" | The people shout, "The gods have come down to us in human form!" and bring a sacrifice to offer. |
| 3. Patron's Response | Herod did not give glory to God, so he dies and was eaten by worms. | The apostles rip their clothes in protest and speak about the benevolent creator. |

**Table 11.2.** Patronage contrasting in Acts

Affluent missionaries can be easily revered as patrons. People wait to shake our hands; families happily welcome us to their homes; government officials make time for us; villagers speak about us in grandiose terms. The preferential treatment feels good and can lead to an inflated self-perception—*my* business employs fifteen families; *I* help people in need; *our* nongovernmental organization supports three hundred farmers. We can easily believe that our generosity proves our noble character. Though no Christian missionary would accept outright worship from beneficiaries, our hearts do find ways to skim a little glory off the top before passing it on to God. We relish the admiration from others or get perturbed when someone fails to recognize our help. This temptation to inflate our self-importance is a great challenge for being a biblical patron. In our public words and in our private thoughts, we must channel all adoration toward God and portray God as the ultimate giver.

The ability to serve as a biblical patron requires a transformation of both the heart and the mind, as we see in the story of Nebuchadnezzar. While strolling atop his royal palace one day, king Nebuchadnezzar of Babylon boasts in his glory, "Is this not magnificent Babylon, which *I* have built as a royal capital by *my* mighty power and for *my* glorious majesty?" (Daniel 4:30, emphasis added). Nebuchadnezzar has a warped view of his role as patron. So God makes him eat grass like a cow, until he learns that "the Most High has sovereignty over the kingdom of mortals and gives it to whom he will" (Daniel 4:32). Nebuchadnezzar eventually acquires a God-centered perspective on wealth, power, and patronage.

> When that period was over, I, Nebuchadnezzar, lifted my eyes to heaven, and my reason returned to me.
> I blessed the Most High,
> and praised and honored the one who lives forever.
> For his sovereignty is an everlasting sovereignty,
> and his kingdom endures from generation to generation. . . .
> Now I, Nebuchadnezzar, praise and extol and honor the King of heaven.
> (Daniel 4:34, 37)

True patronage requires a spiritual transformation, like that of Nebuchadnezzar. False patronage is rooted in spiritual idolatry. Patrons love to "play god." They assume cosmic importance and exalt themselves—"Look at the great kingdom I have built!" When God knocked Nebuchadnezzar off his throne, he finally surrendered and lifted his eyes up to heaven.

Conversion to biblical patronage also requires a new cognitive framework. Nebuchadnezzar himself began praising God as the patron-king after his "reason returned" (Daniel 4:34, 36). Nebuchadnezzar still possesses his royal majesty and glorious kingdom, but comes to understand his royal patronage within the larger context of God's sovereign benefaction. God has ultimate power to provide, so he gets the praise and honor. Our minds must comprehend this fact. In Romans 1:21-22, Paul associates twisted clientage with a darkened mind: "Though they *knew* God, they did not honor him as God or give thanks to him, but they became *futile in their thinking*, and their *senseless minds were darkened*. Claiming to be wise, they became fools" (emphasis added). Corrupted patronage flows from an idolatrous heart and darkened mind. For this reason, biblical patronage only happens as God renews our hearts and minds to perceive the realities of his benevolent graces.

## RECEIVING LIFE

Corrupt patronage is problematic, but so is corrupted clientage. Sinful clients exacerbate unhealthy relationships. Clients who hope in earthly patrons commit idolatry. They trust patrons to solve all their problems. Destitute people cast responsibility upon other people as a way of escape. This may help them survive another day at the patron's hand but leads to the mentality of a helpless victim. Such clients with an entitlement mentality can demand, complain, gossip, and betray to manipulate relationships for material gain.

To transform patronage, clients too must situate the relationship in the broader context of divine patronage. God-honoring clients trust God (not toadyism) for provision and give their ultimate loyalty to Jesus (not human patrons).

The story of Jesus feeding the five thousand people offers an example for transformed clientage. In John 6, large crowds follow Jesus, the famous miracle worker, to acquire more benefits from him. As the evening approaches, Jesus multiplies five loaves and two fish to feed the crowds. This triggers political aspirations among the crowds—if Jesus were their king, all their problems would be fixed! They are ready to abandon other leaders and form an alternative kingdom with Jesus as their provider, protector, and patron (John 6:14-15). Jesus, knowing God's kingdom is different in nature, walks away from the opportunity to become their patron-king.[12]

Jesus did provide bread and genuinely cared about the hungry at first. But when the crowds offer Jesus prestige for more bread, he does not allow the relationship to go down that path. Jesus knows they need more than bread. A full stomach does not change a sinful heart. But the crowds are ignorant of their ultimate need, so they support whichever patron will best guarantee their material needs.

Jesus rebukes the selfish crowd for only wanting material benefits. "Very truly, I tell you, you are looking for me, not because you saw signs, but because you ate your fill of the loaves" (John 6:26). He highlights their deficient, Godless view and challenges their false expectations as clients.

---

[12]These insights on John 6 are adapted from Arley Loewen, "Bread of Life and Patronage" (unpublished notes, n.d.). Used with permission. See also his *Rethinking Honor and Shame* (Micah Network, 2017).

The solution, Jesus tells them, is to acquire the "true bread." He repeatedly points the misguided clients to God's true benefit.

> Do not work for the food that perishes, but for the food that endures for eternal life, which the Son of Man will give you. (John 6:27)

> Very truly, I tell you, it was not Moses who gave you the bread from heaven, but it is my Father who gives you the true bread from heaven. (John 6:32)

> I am the bread of life. Whoever comes to me will never be hungry, and whoever believes in me will never be thirsty. (John 6:35)

> I am the living bread that came down from heaven. Whoever eats of this bread will live forever; and the bread that I will give for the life of the world is my flesh. (John 6:51)

Moses offered manna to the Israelites, but Jesus is superior because he offers the True Bread. He offers patronage far beyond their initial requests. Earthly patrons offer temporary provisions, but Jesus gives eternal life. He satisfies the deepest hungers of our soul by bringing us into God's family. Jesus is not *better* bread, he is the *only* Bread. In John 6, Jesus is the true patron who offers the true patronage that people truly need. This is the benefit that all people must seek.

# 12

# REFRAMING THE
# CHRISTIAN LIFE

A BIBLICAL PARADIGM OF PATRONAGE REFRAMES Christian life and ministry. The previous two chapters discussed how biblical patronage functions in general relationships. This final chapter discusses how patronage impacts five specific areas of the Christian life: spirituality, mission, leadership, discipleship, and community. Although each of these topics warrant a deeper discussion, we simply introduce some ways the framework of patronage can enrich these key areas of the Christian life.

## SPIRITUALITY

Divine patronage transforms our spirituality. Christians who view themselves as God's clients develop a healthy sense of gratitude—a core element of our relationship with God. A thankful heart views all of life as a gift. G. K. Chesterton says, "You say grace before meals. All right. But I say grace before the concert and the opera, and grace before the play and pantomime, and grace before I open a book, and grace before sketching, painting, swimming, fencing, boxing, walking, playing, dancing, and grace before I dip the pen in the ink."[1] Grateful hearts see all the reasons to praise God for his graces, even in difficult seasons.

Thankfulness is foundational in our relationship with God. Joe Carter of the Gospel Coalition explains,

> The regular practice of gratitude is a means by which we become rightly oriented toward God. Only when we become truly grateful for what God has

---

[1] G.K. Chesterton, "A Grace," in *The Collected Works of G.K. Chesterton, Volume X: Collected Poetry Part I*, ed. Aiden Mackey (San Francisco: Ignatius Press, 1994), 43.

done—when thankfulness has seeped into the marrow of our soul—can we fully appreciate who God is and understand who we are as his children.[2]

Our gratitude honors God as the creator and giver of all things. God is the patron; we are the client. He gives grace; we give thanks. This is the core of Christian spirituality.

Gratitude sanctifies our own heart and undercuts sin. Giving thanks opens our own eyes to the magnificence and grandeur of God, the giver of every perfect gift (James 1:17). Gratitude shifts our hearts from being *self*-centered to becoming *God*-exalting. Moreover, as we practice gratitude for God's past graces, we begin to anticipate God's future graces. Rather than fret about the future, our souls hope and trust in God's benevolence (Hebrews 11:1-2). Scientists have also learned how an "attitude of gratitude" has many health benefits, such as mental health, emotional resilience, greater empathy, and better self-esteem.[3] The virtue of thankfulness enhances our quality of life in concrete ways.

Gratitude is itself a gift from God. All creatures enjoy God's blessings, but only humans have the reasoning and imagination to thank God. G. K. Chesterton said, "Thanks are the highest form of thought, and that gratitude is happiness doubled by wonder." Gratitude for grace is yet another grace from our divine Patron.

Gratitude is not a natural habit of the heart. We must practice this spiritual discipline. God's people are commanded to "give thanks in all circumstances; for this is the will of God in Christ Jesus for you" (1 Thessalonians 5:18). There are many ways to incline our hearts towards thankfulness: stopping to "say grace" throughout the day, thanking someone for our relationship with them, or ending the day by recounting what we are grateful for. These practices can cultivate our hearts as loyal, honoring clients.

Thankfulness enhances God's glory and nourishes our soul. But our sin-warped hearts easily turn grace into obligation. Many Christians wrongly

---

[2]Joe Carter, "Why We Should Be Thankful for the Gift of Gratitude," *The Gospel Coalition*, November 19, 2016, www.thegospelcoalition.org/article/why-we-should-be-thankful-for-the-gift-of-gratitude.

[3]Amy Morin, "7 Scientifically Proven Benefits of Gratitude That Will Motivate You to Give Thanks Year-Round," *Forbes*, November 23, 2014, www.forbes.com/sites/amymorin/2014/11/23/7-scientifically-proven-benefits-of-gratitude-that-will-motivate-you-to-give-thanks-year-round/.

receive God's gift of salvation as indentured slaves who must repay a debt. They approach Christian ministry or spiritual disciplines as payments they owe God, but this perverts our spiritual motivation. Living the Christian life as an obligatory repayment nullifies grace and undermines faith. Patronage, when incorrectly applied to our relationship to God, can destroy spiritual vitality. Therefore, we must rightly understand the freeness of God's grace and our true obligation to the Lord Jesus.[4]

Our actions never earn God's blessings or keep us in God's favors. God's salvation is a gift, not wages (Romans 4:4-5). The mere attempt to repay God demeans his benevolent mercy (Matthew 16:21-35). The free gift of God's salvation is an opportunity for a genuine relationship, not a debt-inducing burden.

However, our inability to repay God does *not* mean we owe God nothing. God deserves worship and glory (Romans 11:33-36; 1 Timothy 1:17; Jude 24-25). The king who forgives rebels deserves gratitude. The appropriate response to God's grace "is to offer our whole lives as living sacrifices to our kind Father (Romans 12:1). The focus isn't repaying God, but giving him what he's due from a posture of joy rather than indebtedness."[5] The compulsion to reciprocate God's salvation is healthy when our motivation is to glorify—not repay—God. Christians *should* desire to worship God with their entire lives as a response to his favors. Because Christ has already assumed our infinite honor debt to God, we *should* seek to honor his grace. A biblical theology of grace and divine patronage keeps us from the grace-denying extremes of ungratefulness and repayment.

Our relationship with God could be explained in these terms: God as Patron has demonstrated his faithfulness to us by giving the gift of his Son, and we clients honor him with unflinching loyalty and obedience for his benevolence. Because God has assumed responsibility for our salvation, our lives are committed to his glory. The sole basis of our patron-client relationship with God is his grace—a gift given without any regard to our previous worth or status. God has sovereignly elected us to be recipients of

---

[4]Jeremy Yong, "Why Grace Is Hard for Me as an Asian American," *The Gospel Coalition*, November 17, 2016, www.thegospelcoalition.org/article/why-grace-is-hard-for-me-as-asian-american. These points are adapted from Yong's post.
[5]Yong, "Why Grace Is Hard for Me."

his patronage, called us to praise his lavish generosity, and transformed our hearts to be faithful to him.

## MISSION

Patronage shapes our missional vocation as believers; God's people are brokers who mediate divine favor.[6] Christian ministry is being an honorable mediator of God's salvific blessings. Our connection with the Patron positions us as spiritual brokers. We are "delegate benefactors" who assist God in his global patronage.[7] God's people who receive God's favors must broker God's benefactions for God's glory. This paradigm of mission is a biblical motif, as we see in the lives of Abraham, the Twelve, Paul, and early Christians.

When God called Abraham, he positioned him as a universal broker of divine blessings.[8] God blessed Abraham with family, land, and a great name *so that* all the families of the earth would experience God's favors. God promised to Abraham, "In you all the families of the earth shall be blessed" (Genesis 12:3). The people of Israel, as a "light to the nations," were God's vehicle for mediating his salvation to all peoples.

In the gospels, Jesus called and empowered his disciples to do his work of healing, exorcizing, and teaching (Matthew 10:1-15; Luke 9:1-6). The Twelve mediated the benefactions of Jesus. At first, they acted like typical brokers by regulating access to the patron (Mark 10:13-14) and guarding their own privilege (Mark 9:38-39). But Jesus instructed them to network with the unconnected and to give as a response of having received themselves.[9] Jesus discipled the Twelve to serve as transformed patrons in his Church. After Jesus' ascension the disciples received "power from on high" (Luke 24:49, see Acts 1:8) to do greater works than Jesus (John 14:12-14). In Acts, they mediate Jesus' "benefactions" and broker his salvation (Acts 4:9-12).

---

[6]David deSilva, *Honor, Patronage, Kinship & Purity: Unlocking New Testament Culture* (Downers Grove, IL: IVP Academic, 2000), 138.
[7]Frederick W. Danker, *Luke*, Proclamation Commentaries (Philadelphia: Fortress, 1985), 42-43.
[8]Werner Mischke, *The Global Gospel: Achieving Missional Impact in Our Multicultural World* (Scottsdale, AR: Mission ONE, 2015), 255.
[9]deSilva, *Honor, Patronage, Kinship & Purity*, 138.

The apostle Paul felt "obligated" to serve Gentiles because of the honorable favors he received (Romans 1:14 NIV). The grace of apostleship, while a great privilege, involved the responsibility of mediating divine favor. David deSilva says about Paul, "He presents himself consistently as acting on behalf of the believers, bringing them spiritual blessing, and often incurring great costs and braving great dangers and pains to bring them these benefits."[10] Paul announced the good news that Jesus mediates divine benefactions to all peoples.

The church, like Old Testament Israel, has become God's channel for mediating salvation. Christians are the very means by which God's salvation is realized in the world. We are "vessels" of God's glory, the "body" of Christ, and "ambassadors" of God's righteousness—all metaphors of instrumentality. Through Christians, the world encounters and experiences God's salvation (2 Corinthians 2:14–5:21; Colossians 1:24-29). Brokerage is a vital dimension of our missional vocation. God's people extend God's favors, both spiritual and material.[11] Grace turns us unworthy recipients into mediators. Christians are brokers in the kingdom of God.

## PASTORAL LEADERSHIP

In Majority World contexts, pastors function as patrons. They help church members who expect various forms of patronage: knowledge, counsel, blessing, confirmation of salvation, and even financial help. In return, church members esteem the pastor and submit to his instruction. Erasing all sense of patronage in church communities is neither biblical nor feasible. The real question is this: How will pastors steward their patron-client relationship with other Christians? Will they be worldly patrons or biblical patrons?

Sadly, many pastors in church leadership default to corrupted forms of patronage. They use their authority in domineering ways and undercut emerging leaders to maintain a loyal entourage of church members. The factional competition among pastors for followers breeds division within the

---

[10]deSilva, *Honor, Patronage, Kinship & Purity*, 139.

[11]Early church fathers agree that God's benevolence is the source and motivating factor for Christian ministry in the world. Alan B. Wheatley, *Patronage in Early Christianity: Its Use and Transformation from Jesus to Paul of Samosata* (Eugene, OR: Wipf & Stock Pub, 2011).

church. Pastors may suppress criticism of themselves but then harshly rebuke others. Such leaders imitate what they have seen—corrupted patronage.

The Bible instructs church leaders to be benevolent patrons who "shepherd the flock." Shepherds guide, nurture, and protect their flocks. Note the language of patronage/shepherding in Paul's admonition to the Ephesian church leaders, "*Keep watch* over yourselves and over all the *flock*, of which the Holy Spirit has made you *overseers*, to *shepherd* the church of God" (Acts 20:28, emphasis added). Using similar imagery, Peter exhorts church elders

> to tend [lit. "shepherd"] the flock of God that is in your charge, exercising the oversight, not under compulsion but willingly, as God would have you do it—not for sordid gain but eagerly. Do not lord it over those in your charge, but be examples to the flock. And when the chief shepherd appears, you will win the crown of glory that never fades away. (1 Peter 5:2-4)

The natural tendency of patron-leaders, even within the household of God, is to exact personal gain and lord over inferiors. Knowing these common temptations, Peter explicitly tells the leaders to not lead the flock of God in this manner.

The elders should instead tend the flock and exercise oversight "as God would have you do it" and as "examples to the flock." These instructions reframe leadership. Pastors should view their patronage relationships from the perspectives of God and the client, not their own vantage point. The phrase "as God would have you do it" introduces God's perspective on patron-leadership. How would God have them exercise oversight? What does God desire from Christian pastors? Merely asking these questions leans into a God-centered approach to patronage. The second admonition to "be examples to the flock" reminds leaders that they must be the type of patron they would desire to follow. This suggests a Golden Rule for patronage: "Treat your clients as you want your patrons to treat you."

To transform leadership at the heart level, people must address the main motive that propels patronage—glory and honor. Instead of condemning leaders' desire for honor, Peter redefines the nature of honor. Elders who lead benevolently "will win the crown of glory that never fades away" when Jesus returns. The reward for shepherding comes from the Chief Shepherd, not from the sheep. Pastors lead and serve without considering how they stand to benefit in this age, knowing they will win a glorious crown in the age to come. Eternal glory propels virtuous patronage.

A patron's honor is based on virtue and service, not domination and control. Virtuous leaders hold status with an open hand, not a clenched fist. They give rather than grasp. This open-handed approach to leadership dismantles the entrenched system of power hoarding. Larry Persons describes the character of benevolent patrons:

> They emphasize inner goodness rather than outward appearance. They do good for the sake of good itself, not as a show. They are other-centered, not self-centered. They avoid problems by separating personal relationships from the duties they are bound to perform. They can be trusted to be fair. They nurture subordinates and take joy in their successes. They do not cheat, swindle, or exploit others. They genuinely care about what benefits the collective—solving problems and improving the lives of others.[12]

## DISCIPLESHIP

Christians might leverage patronage to cultivate a deeper relationship with disciples. In patronage relationships, clients become more open to spiritual influence. Patronage creates discipleship opportunities for transmitting Christian values to spiritual "children" (cf. 1 Corinthians 4:15). After researching African leadership, missionary Del Chinchen identifies patronage as the "indigenous style of discipleship practiced naturally by many national leaders."[13] Patronage can be leveraged to develop true, substantive relationships between disciplers and disciplees. When cultural awareness and spiritual maturity are present, "trust, respect, love and other affective ties begin to pervade the relationship, setting into motion a pattern that builds in momentum."[14] This produces an enduring, intimate patron-client relationship that is conducive to genuine discipleship.

---

[12]Larry Persons, *The Way Thais Lead: Face as Social Capital* (Chiang Mai, Thailand: Silkworm Books, 2016), chapter 20.

[13]Delbert Chinchen, "The Patron-Client System: A Model of Indigenous Discipleship," *EMQ* 31, no. 4 (Oct 1995), missionexus.org/the-patron-client-system-a-model-of-indigenous-discipleship/.

[14]Chinchen, "Patron-Client System"; Delbert Chinchen, "The Patron-Client Relationship Concept: A Case Study from the African Bible Colleges in Liberia and Malawi" (unpublished PhD diss., Biola

Mixing discipleship and patronage can be dangerous, so one must be mindful and cautious. In the history of Christian missions, patronage dynamics have produced many "rice Christians"—people who profess to be Christian for material benefits rather than genuine spiritual reasons. Such nominal Christians agree to anything a patron says to get help, food, or medical benefits. Short-term mission trips are most vulnerable to this reality. Being oblivious to patronage dynamics, they misinterpret the response of the client-recipients.

Patronage dynamics can also warp relationships between expatriate missions and local pastors. Robert Oh examines this danger in his article "Patron-Client Dynamics Between Korean Missionaries and Cambodian Christians." Cambodian Christians in one city "were offered church planting positions from major denominations in Korea, such as Baptists, Methodists, and Presbyterians. They were approached by individual Korean missionaries and offered different salary scales. However, during this process, mistrust and infighting actually ended up in fistfights between the Cambodian Christians."15 Korean missionaries were in effect buying churches for their denominations, and Cambodian pastors were selling their congregation to the highest bidder. In these warped "discipleship relationships," both sides manipulated the system of patronage and used each other. The outside patrons got the numbers of ministry success they wanted, and the local clients got the material provisions they wanted. There was little sense of a genuine relationship. The arrangement was instrumental, and the bond was light. This pseudo-patronage was neither God-centered nor life-giving. For discipleship relationships to be truly Christian, they must display ever-increasing aspects of biblical patronage, which we have defined as being God-centered and life-giving.

## COMMUNITY

Divine patronage provides a new paradigm for community relationships. God's people, having freely received God's favor, freely extend God's grace

---

University, 1994), 225.

[15]Robert Oh, "Patron-Client Dynamics Between Korean Missionaries and Cambodian Christians," *Asia Missions Advance* 48 (July 2015): 14.

to others. The cross redefines gifts, wealth, reciprocity, patronage, and clientage for the edification of the community.

This new community ethic guards against using patronage in a utilitarian manner. The apostle James wrote to believers who had a dysfunctional view of patronage. Poor and rich Christians manipulated the social hierarchy for selfish gain. Poor Christians flattered the rich to curry favor. At church gatherings, they offered seats of honor to those wearing fine clothes and made poor people sit on the floor. James denounces this favoritism (James 2:1-12). Such manipulative behavior: (1) proves partial people are in fact judges with evil thoughts (James 2:4), (2) dishonors the poor whom God has chosen to inherit the kingdom (James 2:5-6), (3) exalts their oppressors who blaspheme God's name (James 2:6-7), and (4) makes them transgressors of God's law (James 2:8-12). Giving preference to richer Christians during church gatherings in order to curry favor perverts God's design for community. Then James 5:1-6 denounces oppressive patrons. The rich fraudulently withheld wages from their laborers. Such injustices invoke future miseries and cause their wealth to dissolve into nothing. Wealthy Christians who exploit people in need fail to steward their wealth for the common good. Their behavior prohibits genuine community and flourishing relationships.

As a counterpoint to the blatant partiality and oppressive patronage practiced in the church, James portrays God as an ideal benefactor for all Christians. Amidst trials and challenges, God gives generously (James 1:5-8). The "Father of lights" is a loyal and unchanging provider who gives "every good and perfect gift" (James 1:17 ESV). Our relationship with God is one of friendship—an ancient euphemism for patronage (James 2:23; 4:4). And God extends favors and exaltation to those who are humble (James 4:6).[16] In James, God is a faithful benefactor.

Believers should resist overdependence upon wealthy leaders and instead trust in the benefits of God. Material needs in the community are then met as believers extend beneficence to one another. These acts of generosity (James 2:15-17) and hospitality (James 2:25) prove the genuineness of one's

---

[16]Alicia Batten, "God in the Letter of James: Patron or Benefactor?," *NTS* 50 (2004): 268. This paragraph summarizes Batten's article.

faith. God's benevolence transforms community life. The giving and receiving of grace *in Christ* reconfigures reality and remakes community. Su-
pernatural grace makes the church an alternate "network of friends" who
delegate access to God's power and provision.

Jesus' model of transformed patronage shapes the new community
so that giving resources does not translate into special honors
(cf. Acts 2:43-47; 4:32-37). Believers share as equal members within God's
family. People give to meet a need, not to receive honor or garner loyalty.
Christian patronage reflects God's benevolence. Such grace disregards
worldly criteria of worth and status.[17] God's generosity transforms reciprocal relationships, motivating us to "live in love, as Christ loved us and
gave himself up for us" (Ephesians 5:2).

## CONCLUSION

Throughout history, God and his people have leveraged patronage for the
purposes of his kingdom. Patronage has a biblical precedent and informs
key elements of the gospel and Christian ministry.

Patronage can be a fruitful model of establishing genuine relationships,
discipling believers, and mediating grace. But in a fallen world, there are
many snares in patronage relationships. When you combine money, honor,
and relationships, life gets messy (especially in crosscultural situations). Sin
does indeed pervert patronage into manipulative or oppressive relationships.

Nevertheless God calls people to a new, transformed patronage, characterized as God-centered and life-giving. Christians engage others through
this alternative paradigm. Patron-client relationships, redefined by the cross,
become a structure for mutual giving and generosity.

This book offers only an introduction to patronage. Many issues, both
theological and practical, deserve more attention. Since patronage dynamics are unique in each context, local conversations are perhaps the best
path towards a better understanding of patronage. Context matters, and
we must account for that reality. Also, the conversation about patronage is

---

[17]John Barclay, "Grace and the Countercultural Reckoning of Worth: Community Construction of
Galatians 5-6," in *Galatians and Christian Theology: Justification, the Gospel, and Ethics in Paul's Letter*,
ed. N. T. Wright et al. (Grand Rapids: Baker Academic, 2014), 573.

often from the perspective of patrons, but numerically more people are clients than patrons. How can we hear from clients on this topic? Likewise, many books on patronage are written by men, so the discussion focuses on only half of the population. How do patronage relationships function among women? The voices of clients and women offer a wealth of potential insights to consider. Finally, we must continue to examine how Western (non-patronage) cultural assumptions shape our hermeneutics and theology. I have made a few proposals regarding how patronage aids our interpretation of biblical texts and Christian theology. Also, this book applies biblical patronage mostly to global missions and crosscultural relationships, but there are many other settings where patronage dynamics need to be examined (e.g., urban ministry, political leadership). These are just a few important ways the conversation on patronage can move forward.

May God's Spirit lead you into a deeper knowledge of his benevolent grace and equip you to mediate that grace to others in a God-exalting and life-giving way. May you live by the grace of God and for the glory of God.

# APPENDIX 1

*Further Resources*

This bibliography includes works for further understanding patronage. Publications are organized by their primary emphasis.

## OLD TESTAMENT STUDIES

Georges, Jayson. *Psalms: An Honor-Shame Paraphrase of 15 Psalms*. Timē Press, 2017.

Lemche, Niels Peter. "Kings and Clients: On Loyalty Between the Ruler and the Ruled in Ancient 'Israel.'" *Semeia* 66 (1994): 119-32.

Levenson, Jon. *The Love of God: Divine Gift, Human Gratitude, and Mutual Faithfulness in Judaism*. Princeton, NJ: Princeton University Press, 2015.

Moran, William. "Ancient Near Eastern Background of the Love of God in Deuteronomy." *Catholic Biblical Quarterly* 25, no. 1 (1963): 77-87.

Simkins, Ronald. "Patronage and the Political Economy of Monarchic Israel." *Semeia* 87 (1999): 123-44.

Tucker Jr., W. Dennis. "Is Shame a Matter of Patronage in the Communal Laments?" *Journal for the Study of the Old Testament* 31, no. 4 (2007): 465-80.

Westbrook, Raymond. "Patronage in the Ancient Near East." *Journal of the Economic and Social History of the Orient* 48, no. 2 (2005): 210-233.

## NEW TESTAMENT STUDIES

Barclay, John. *Paul and the Gift*. Grand Rapids: Eerdmans, 2015.

Batten, Alicia. "God in the Letter of James: Patron or Benefactor?" *New Testament Studies* 50 (2004): 257-72.

Briones, David. *Paul's Financial Policy: A Socio-Theological Approach*. London: Bloomsbury T&T Clark, 2015.

Campbell, Joan Cecelia. *Phoebe: Patron and Emissary*. Collegeville, MN: Liturgical Press, 2009.

Chow, John. *Patronage and Power: A Study of Social Networks in Corinth.* Sheffield, England: Bloomsbury T&T Clark, 1992.

Crook, Zeba. *Reconceptualising Conversion: Patronage, Loyalty, and Conversion in the Religions of the Ancient Mediterranean.* New York: De Gruyter, 2004.

Danker, Frederick. *Benefactor: Epigraphic Study of a Graeco-Roman and New Testament Semantic Field.* St. Louis, MO: Clayton Publishing House, 1982.

deSilva, David. "Patronage & Grace in the New Testament," Chap. 4 in *Honor, Patronage, Kinship & Purity: Unlocking New Testament Culture.* Downers Grove, IL: IVP Academic, 2000.

_____. "Exchanging Favor for Wrath: Apostasy in Hebrews and Patron-Client Relationships." *Journal of Biblical Literature* 115 (1996): 91-116.

_____. "'We Are Debtors': Grace and Obligation in Paul and Seneca." In *Paul and Seneca in Dialogue*, edited by Joseph Dodson and David Briones, 150-78. Leiden: Brill, 2017.

Downs, David. "Is God Paul's Patron? The Economy of Patronage in Pauline Theology." In *Engaging Economics: New Testament Scenarios and Early Christian Reception*, edited by Bruce Longenecker and Kelley Liebengood, 129-56. Grand Rapids: Eerdmans, 2009.

Elliott, J. H. "Patronage and Clientism in Early Christian Society: A Short Reading Guide." *Forum* 3 (1987): 39-48.

Harrison, James. *Paul's Language of Grace in Its Graeco-Roman Context.* Tübingen: Mohr Siebeck, 2003.

Joshua, Nathan Mzyoko. *Benefaction and Patronage in Leadership: A Socio-Historical Exegesis of the Pastoral Epistles.* Carlisle, UK: Langham Monographs, 2018.

Joubert, Stephan. *Paul as Benefactor: Reciprocity, Strategy and Theological Reflection in Paul's Collection.* Eugene, OR: Wipf and Stock, 2016.

Marshall, Jonathan. *Jesus, Patrons, and Benefactors: Roman Palestine and the Gospel of Luke.* Eugene, OR: Wipf and Stock, 2015.

Moxnes, Halvor. "Patron-Client Relations and the New Community in Luke-Acts." In *The Social World of Luke-Acts*, edited by Jerome H. Neyrey, 241-66. Grand Rapids: Baker Academic, 1999.

Neyrey, Jerome H. "God, Benefactor and Patron: The Major Cultural Model for Interpreting the Deity in Greco-Roman Antiquity." *Journal for the Study of the New Testament* 27, no. 4 (June 2005): 465-92.

Piper, Ronald. "Glory, Honor, and Patronage in the Fourth Gospel: Understanding the 'Doxa' Given to Disciples in John 17." In *Social Scientific Models for Interpreting the Bible: Essays by the Context Group in Honor of Bruce J. Malina*, edited by John Pilch, 281-309. Boston: Brill, 2001.

Richards, Randolph, and Brandon O'Brien. "First Things First: Rules and Relationships," Chap. 7 in *Misreading Scripture with Western Eyes: Removing Cultural
Blinders to Better Understand the Bible*. Downers Grove, IL: InterVarsity Press, 2012.

Wheatley, Alan. *Patronage in Early Christianity: Its Use and Transformation from
Jesus to Paul of Samosata*. Eugene, OR: Wipf & Stock, 2011.

Winter, Bruce. *Seek the Welfare of the City: Christians as Benefactors and Citizens*.
Grand Rapids: Eerdmans, 1994.

## ANTHROPOLOGICAL AND CLASSICAL STUDIES

Dio, Chrysostomus. *Discourses* 31-36. The Loeb Classical Library vol. 358. Translated by James Wilfred Cohoon and Henry Lamar Crosby. Cambridge: Harvard
University Press, 1940.

Eilers, Claude. *Roman Patrons of Greek Cities*. Oxford Classical Monographs.
Oxford: Oxford University Press, 2002.

Eisenstadt, S. R., and L. Roniger. *Patrons, Clients and Friends: Interpersonal Relations
and the Structure of Trust in Society*. Cambridge: Cambridge University Press, 1984.

Saller, Richard P. *Personal Patronage Under the Early Empire*. Cambridge: Cambridge University Press, 1982.

Seneca, Lucius Annaeus. *On Benefits*. The Complete Works of Lucius Annaeus
Seneca. Translated by Miriam Griffin and Brad Inwood. Chicago: University
of Chicago Press, 2011.

Verboven, Koenraad. *The Economy of Friends: Economic Aspects of* Amicitia *and
Patronage in the Late Republic*. Brussels: Latomus, 2002.

Wolf, Eric R. "Kinship, Friendship, and Patron-Client Relations in Complex Societies." In *The Social Anthropology of Complex Societies*, edited by M. Banton,
1-22. London: Tavistock, 1966.

For an annotated bibliography of academic works on patronage, see Zeba Crook's
online article "Patronage/Benefaction" available at www.oxfordbibliographies
.com/view/document/obo-9780195393361/obo-9780195393361-0203.xml.

## MISSIOLOGY

Chinchen, Delbert. "The Patron-Client System: A Model of Indigenous Discipleship." *Evangelical Missions Quarterly* 31, no. 4 (October 1995).

_____. "The Return of the Fourth 'R' to Education: Relationships," *Missiology: An
International Review* 25, no. 3 (July 1997): 321-35.

Crouch, Andy. *Strong and Weak*. Downers Grove, IL: IVP Books, 2016.

Dale, Morya. "Who Has Bewitched You: Patronage, Blessing, and the Evil Eye,"
*When Women Speak* 3, no. 1 (Sept 2018): 55-81.

DeNeui, Paul. "Speaking of the Unspeakable: Money and Missions in Patron-Client Buddhist Cultures." In *Complexities of Money and Mission in Asia*, edited by Paul DeNeui, 105-20. Pasadena, CA: William Carey Library, 2012.

Edwards, Colin. "Patronage, Salvation, and Being Joined with Jesus: Socio-Anthropological Insights from South Asia." Chap. 9 in *Longing for Community: Church, Ummah, or Somewhere in Between?*, ed. David Greenlee. Pasadena, CA: William Carey Library, 2013.

Maranz, David. *African Friends and Money Matters: Observations from Africa.* Dallas, TX: SIL International, 2001.

Oh, Robert. "Patron-Client Dynamics Between Korean Missionaries and Cambodian Christians." *Asia Missions Advance* 48 (July 2015): 12-19.

Persons, Larry. *The Way Thais Lead: Face as Social Capital.* Chiang Mai, Thailand: Silkworm Books, 2016.

Shaw, Perry. "Patronage, Exemption, and Institutional Policy." *Evangelical Missions Quarterly* 49, no. 1 (January 2013): 8-13.

Tito, James. "A Lesson from Jose: Understanding the Patron/Client Relationship." *Evangelical Missions Quarterly* 44, no. 3 (July 2008).

The Patronage Symposium (October 2018, Beirut), gathering practitioners and scholars to discuss a biblical missiology of patronage. Audio recordings of the twenty presentations are available through honorshame.com/patsym-presentations.

## BOOKS ABOUT MISSIONS AND MONEY IN GENERAL

Bonk, Jonathan J. *Missions and Money: Affluence as a Missionary Problem . . . Revisited.* Revised and expanded edition. Maryknoll, NY: Orbis Books, 2007.

Corbett, Steve and Brian Fikkert. *When Helping Hurts: How to Alleviate Poverty Without Hurting the Poor . . . and Yourself.* Chicago: Moody Publishers, 2014.

Lederleitner, Mary T. *Cross-Cultural Partnerships.* Downers Grove, IL: InterVarsity Press, 2010.

Lupton, Robert D. *Toxic Charity: How Churches and Charities Hurt Those They Help, and How to Reverse It.* New York: HarperOne, 2012.

Reese, Robert. *Roots and Remedies of the Dependency Syndrome in World Missions.* Pasadena, CA: William Carey Library, 2010.

Schwartz, Glenn J. *When Charity Destroys Dignity: Overcoming Unhealthy Dependency in the Christian Movement.* Bloomington, IN: AuthorHouse, 2007.

Shaw, Karen. *Wealth and Piety: Middle Eastern Perspectives for Expat Workers.* Littleton, CO: William Carey Publishing, 2018.

# APPENDIX 2

## Discussion and Reflection Questions

### Part I: Cultural Issues

- How would you explain patron-client relationships to someone in your context (avoiding technical terms)? What specific words or metaphors express the idea?

- What are some examples of patronage, both from your personal life and from the broader culture?

- How do you respond when you sense the expectations of patronage?

- How does this book portray and evaluate the system of patronage? Do you agree the author's assessment?

- What else would you like to learn about patronage?

### Part II: Biblical Models

- How did patronage shape Yahweh's covenant relationship with Israel?

- How does Jesus' role as a patron in the Gospels affect our relationship with him now?

- How can Paul's examples help you better navigate patronage cultures?

- How would you summarize Yahweh's, Jesus', and Paul's response to patronage?

- What is your response to this statement—"Patronage is not a biblical concept?"

### Part III: Theological Concepts

- What do you think of this statement—"God is a patron"? Explain your response.

- How does understanding sin as "relational disloyalty" or "client ingratitude" help our spiritual transformation and sanctification?
- Of the explanations for salvation, grace, faith, conversion, and the atonement, which one(s) did you find most helpful?
- How might you present the gospel differently in patronage contexts?
- How would you compare and contrast the theology presented in chapters 7–9 with your previous theological understandings?

## Part IV: Missional Applications

- How might you leverage patronage in your relationships? How might you be a better patron or client? Give specific examples.
- Describe someone who seems to be a good, benevolent patron?
- What are specific ways you can make your reciprocal relationships more God-centered and life-giving?
- What is the biggest challenge of patron-client relationships?
- How does patronage affect your view of the Christian life and ministry?

# GENERAL INDEX

Paul the apostle, 135, 138-39, 147
peacemaking 123-26
Pharisees, 56-57
Philippines, 123-25
*philotimia*, 14
Phinehas, 45
Phoebe, 73-74
politics. *See* government
reciprocity, 10-11, 14, 16, 35, 63, 98, 117, 118, 135-36
relationship, 10, 29-30, 32, 116-18
Russian, 117
Seneca, 16, 20, 88
sacrifices, 43-45
salvation, 97, 107
shame. *See* honor and shame

Shweder, Richard, 16
sin, 14, 83, 88-89, 94-95, 107, 140
social capital, 11-12
Soviet Union, 20-21
spirituality, 143-46
stewardship, 129-30
suzerain-vassal, 40-42
teaching, 121-22
thankfulness. *See* gratitude
Watson, Thomas, 95
Western perception, 1-2, 29-31, 126
Winter, Bruce, 72-72
wisdom, 49
work relationships, 121
wrath, 94
Yahweh. *See* God

# SCRIPTURE INDEX

# ALSO AVAILABLE

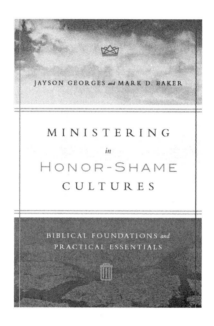

For more resources and training materials about patronage,
visit the webpage honorshame.com/patronage.